THE INSTITUTE OF POLITICS PUBLICATIONS
WILLIAMS COLLEGE, WILLIAMSTOWN, MASS.

DIPLOMATIC EUROPE SINCE THE TREATY OF VERSAILLES

DIPLOMATIC EUROPE

SINCE THE

TREATY OF VERSAILLES

BY

COUNT CARLO SFORZA

MEMBER OF ITALIAN SENATE AND FORMERLY MINISTER
FOR FOREIGN AFFAIRS

NEW HAVEN
PUBLISHED FOR THE INSTITUTE OF POLITICS
BY THE YALE UNIVERSITY PRESS
LONDON · HUMPHREY MILFORD · OXFORD UNIVERSITY PRESS
MCMXXVIII

PREFACE

It needed but a few chapters to give the impression that this book was a complete survey of the illusions and disillusions, the fevered strivings and the sterile struggles, which went to form the travail of European international life after the Great War.

I have purposely refrained from writing these chapters, chiefly because I did not wish to touch, here, upon questions and episodes which might have led to the discussion of ideas or pretended ideas upon which, in other fields, I have openly expressed my thought. Moreover, apart from any such personal feeling, it seemed to me premature, and therefore useless, to attempt to paint a general picture of the whole; the postwar history of Europe is still in the making. I have wished merely to add an historical contribution to that ensemble, by recording the aspect and the trend of some events to which I could partly bear personal witness.

Such as they are, these pages do not seek to conceal, although they may not proclaim, the political and moral ideals which were, and remain, my own.

Undoubtedly, those who bear political responsibility for a great country are not entitled to call themselves exclusively the servants of a moral ideal. History sometimes is an iron task-mistress. It suffices—but this is imperative—to direct one's country's interests along the channel marked out for the life of the nations—of the living nations—and not to mistake for that channel certain turbid eddies which for a short space of time flow backward between slimy banks.

In spite of checks and obstacles, we are marching
forward toward a future of European unity. If proof
of this were needed, it would be furnished by the hys-
teria, half real and half assumed, of shortsighted
materialistic interests, afraid of losses on the exchange, with no more insight than the innkeepers
and postilions shouting in the 'Forties against the
construction of railways. Their threats, their hate
propaganda barely veil their sense of forthcoming
defeat.

Thus it has always been in this old world of ours.
When great national entities have been on the point
of coalescing, interprovincial hatreds seemed to
reach their highest paroxysm. At the very moment
when wars of religion were about to vanish forever,
it seemed as though theological strife had never been
so acute. The French terrorists gave the impression
that their riot of carnage would never cease, just
when the atmosphere was on the point of lightening,
and life about to become more smiling and humane.

A century ago, kept in ward on an Atlantic island,
he who had caused the blood of half Europe to flow
in sixty battles, knew a moment of sincerity—unique
in his genius-comedian's career. This was not when
he dictated the Memorial of St. Helena, which was a
statement for the defense—nor yet his Will, a set-
piece for the French people—but when, on the very
eve of his death, he summoned his last strength to
send a final message to his son, with advice drawn
from his unparalleled reserve of experience. On that
occasion Bonaparte was, for once, sincere.

Italian, Corsican, as he had always remained beneath his French veneer, this man was too deeply imbued with family feeling not to be absolutely genuine

with the one human being he truly loved, his son and
heir.

He wrote: "The aim of all my son's efforts should
be, to rule by peace. For the future there is only one
way to convince Europe, and that is, through reason.
My son should be a man of new ideas. . . . The new
idea is, to reunite Europe in the bonds of an indis-
soluble federation. It is in this direction that Europe
is advancing. To endeavor to retard progress would
be a waste of strength. It is useless to struggle
against the inevitable. I cut the Gordian Knot of the
nations; now it must be untied."

So wrote the dying man. To repeat Bonaparte's
phrase, the Gordian Knot of the nations was untied
as a result of the Great War which (in seeming only)
has given the lie to the Corsican's opinion. Indeed,
the World War will one day appear merely as the
culminating proof that we had come to the end of a
Europe thinking of being able to live outside some
more or less loose federal bond.

For all the transitory inconveniences which the
liberation of nationalities must entail, what matters
most is that the natural and permanent materials exist henceforth of a new organized Europe. That these
materials have been created, constitutes the redeem-
ing point of the Versailles Treaty.

Before the War, there was but one guarantee of a
common European existence—the equilibrium of the
Great Powers. The folly of 1914 has proved such an
equilibrium to be no more than a perilous scaffolding
—perilous because artificial.

CARLO SFORZA.

Syosset, Long Island,
    April, 1928.

CONTENTS

DIPLOMATIC EUROPE

I

FRANCE AND GERMANY

I WANT to examine with you certain outstanding moral moments and historical episodes in international European intercourse in the years immediately following the signature of the Versailles Treaty, and to try to draw from them some lasting conclusions and, if possible, some general previsions. The events and feelings I am going to deal with still belong to our contemporary history. But I hope never to lose the only merit I would like to attain for my lectures: candid and serene sincerity. When, during the course of our gatherings, I am reluctantly obliged to quote my own action or personal recollections, it will merely be as a witness. To act otherwise, and to commit the sin so common to all politicians—that is, to speak of oneself—would be, here in this highly intellectual atmosphere, more than indiscreet, almost disrespectful to you. You see that even the only merit I claim for my lectures draws probably its main source from you, my American hearers.

One who attended the Paris negotiations for the Treaty of Versailles and, as in my case, the odd dozen of peripatetic meetings of the Supreme Council which, from Boulogne to Spa, from London to Cannes, added codicils to and experimented with variations of that treaty—such an one may well say that he assisted at the Biblical spectacle of the Tower

of Babel. The meaning of that symbolical myth will
be illuminated for him with a fresh light. Probably
the Asiatic Tower of Babel was less babelesque than
ours, since, as the Bible tells us, the confusion of
tongues was complete. At any rate, in the Chaldean
plains they had this advantage, that nobody could
pretend he was understanding anybody else, and this
negative knowledge was something gained.

What made the post-Versailles period morally
worse, when the Allies remained technically the
Allies, but differed profoundly in aims and ideas,
was that all tried to retain in use the same catch-
words: liberty, independence of peoples, guardianship of the peace, and the like. Alas, each of these
had a different meaning according to the national
language in which it was spoken. Even the word
"Allies" had a doubtful meaning. It implied, in
reality, a lot of governments suspicious of each
other (as, for that matter, has always happened
after a long coalition), a group of States obliged to
remain "the Allies" since a convention signed in
London on September 4, 1914, forced them to keep
their bond while an enemy remained. And this theo-
retical enemy remained (the Turk) not because we
were fighting him, but simply because we never managed to find, between allies, a common formula for
peace. It was their disagreement, not their union,
that forced the Allies to remain allies. That was why
the confusion of language was so tragic, or tragic
and comical at once, in old Europe.

It has become the fashion among those writers
who criticize with most asperity the Treaty of Versailles to discover and to lay stress on the wisdom
and generosity of the Treaty of Vienna which, a cen-

tury before, ended the Napoleonic wars. In truth, such praise has always seemed to me touched with unreality, as always happens when one has recourse to historical analogies. The work of the Congress of Vienna having been directed toward the restoration of old dynasties and the preservation of small artificial states, consequently crushing the aspiring nationalities, especially the Italian and German, could only be transitory, as reactionary and unnatural schemes are bound to be.

When, half a century later, the Italian provisions of the Treaty of Vienna were destroyed (I quote the Italian provisions as they were at once the most typical and essential part of the treaty), the same powers which had arranged together an artificial division of my country, a division which, in their shortsighted views, ought to have guaranteed European stability, suddenly made a discovery. They discovered that the disappearance of their Viennese work, far from endangering a real order, had eliminated from the very heart of Europe an always recrudescent cause of wars, and had at the same time eliminated misleading advantages for some, onerous duties and anxieties for others. All of them found themselves, after 1860,—the date of Italian unification,—much nearer the real equilibrium they had vainly tried to create in Vienna, when they had built on the quicksands of artificial diplomacy, with no concern for the national realities which had matured during the hard travail of the revolutionary years.

In spite, therefore, of brilliant analogies, more literary than real, I cannot agree with the rehabilitation of the Vienna Congress, though it has found two apologists even in Italy, the land which suffered so greatly from that treaty, one of those apologists being the former Prime Minister Nitti, and the other the profound historian of old Rome, Ferrero.

What I have said so far may seem a digression. But I wish to point out as being intimately connected with the study of the post-Versailles period the two typical and antithetical cases in which, in one instance, Vienna surpassed Versailles, and, in the other, Versailles was morally far ahead of Vienna.

The point where Vienna scores is the wise generosity displayed by the victors toward vanquished France. You know this as well as I do; yet I am acquainted with no recent writings which reproduce, in complete antithesis to the decisions of Versailles, a document which seems the most conclusive. I mean the message issued by the Emperor of Russia on March 31, 1814, in the conquered enemy capital, Paris. This message says: "The conditions of peace were meant to contain stronger guarantees, when the question at stake was the suppression of Bonaparte's ambitions. When, as now, France, resuming a wise government, offers an additional guarantee of peace, those conditions must be much more merciful to her." The Emperor Alexander, after affirming that the Allied Governments would respect French integrity, went on to say: "The Allies may go still farther, since it is necessary for the good of Europe that France should remain strong and great." Here indeed we have a language which finds no echo in Paris in 1919, although the *dossiers* of the officials at the Quai d'Orsay, the French Foreign Office, are all overflowing with historic precedents, a fact which, may we note, is not always conducive to the quick appreciation of realities by the French.

The point where, as I told you, Versailles seems to me morally so far ahead of Vienna, is one which has been sharply criticized, especially by diplomats, one which makes this treaty so full of contradictions and dubious alternatives. Those contradictions explain the hesitating experiences of European diplomacy in the years immediately following the treaty. They were an actual cause of disturbance and feebleness. But, when we look at the whole with an historical mind, they really constitute a mark of moral elevation, and a possible way to a future better peace.

The Versailles Treaty might be compared, in due measure, to a bronze statue, in whose composition two gangs of workmen contributed at the moment of fusion, each working independently and each provided with quite different materials to be thrown into the melting. At the fusion moment, the workmen have to act as quickly as possible. So did the negotiators of Versailles who agreed in one point only— that of haste.

But an initial difficulty held them back. The Treaty of Vienna had been speeded up by the fact that the armistice convention which had ended the hostilities after Napoleon's defeat could be regarded as a genuine preliminary peace, so identical were the principles first indicated therein with those of the subsequent treaty. On the other hand, in the discussion which succeeded the Great War, nothing was more irksome to some of the negotiating powers than the recollection that the basis of the armistice with Germany had been indeed no less than Wilson's fourteen points. The remembrance of this was so embarrassing that some wished to forget it; and I really believe that they succeeded in doing so. Such is human na-

ture, so marvelously resourceful is it when it wants
to lull itself in oblivion. Maybe life would otherwise
be unendurable.

Haste being imperative, and the sole point in
which the negotiators were in complete accord, they
strung together article after article, chapter after
chapter, even ones which were often diametrically
opposed to each other. Hence ensued a treaty that
for lack of moral unity, the only unity which has real
permanent results, was bound to appear, especially
to an essentially *raisonneur* people like the French,
illogical by reason of its contradictions, its occasion-
ally vague clauses, its more or less voluntary *lacunae*.

For my part I cannot help seeing something of
tragic and pathetic beauty in the stand made by one
of the Paris negotiators against all the rest, who,
either from motives of vengeance or fear or spirit of
compromise, admitted huckstering formulae, and
who were only too glad to have a reason, later on, for
asking and getting equally tawdry advantages for
themselves. This solitary man, who lived the whole
tragedy with his soul as well as with the life he lost
soon afterward, was forcibly obliged to associate
himself with the incoherence of Versailles. Moreover, when he stiffened to his original intentions, as,
for example, in the question of Fiume, he was making perhaps a graver tactical mistake than by giving
way. A great European people could not see why
such intransigence was to be used against them
alone, and their determination to guard the Italian
character of that small town was only increased
thereby.

The more the solitary figure yielded to exigencies

of the moment, the greater grew his determination
to create a line of escape and a hope of revision, by
means of the League of Nations, at all the turning
points of the treaty. He signed provisory laws to the
relief of politicians who could not see beyond the
present or who expected to confine the future in the
narrow limits of the present. But at the same time he
signed those laws, he forced his colleagues to sign
with him a provision for an outlet which would lead
some day to the revision of what he deemed transitory compromise.

The work and the thought of this man are still
subject for the polemics of the historian, perhaps
even more in this country than elsewhere. But as a
foreigner, whose country of all others might seem
entitled to bear a grudge against him, allow me to
acknowledge in his solitary struggle toward his solitary aims a greatness which bears testimony to the
moral greatness of his race.

For the world to see the utility of these loopholes
to necessary revisions, time, the inexorable force of
time, was wanted; some sterile experiences, like that
of the Ruhr, were probably needed. On the morrow
of Versailles it was no use to hope that minds still
poisoned by the sufferings of the War could envisage
the practical application of the Wilsonian part of the
treaty. Corrections were not yet possible. All that
was generally felt at that time was the disadvantage
of a treaty full of reservations and contradictions.

After the Treaty of Vienna, it had been compara-
tively easy for statesmen and diplomats to work
together. That treaty was concluded between an anti-
Bonapartist European coalition and a France herself become anti-Bonapartist. The same was true

after the Peace of Prague signed in 1866 between Prussia and Austria. From such treaties of peace, those quoted being but two examples out of many, could result only a period of collaboration and of understanding between the signatories.

The Peace of Versailles, by reason of the innate contradiction that I have pointed out, did, it is true, seal the triumph of the victors, but left the one of them nearest to Germany with the bitter sensation that this triumph was transitory, that victory would have to be rewon over and over again. It was a situation to which one needed to become accustomed. In course of time it might have been possible to see its advantages. But the years immediately following the treaty held for those at the head of European affairs nothing but uncertainty, equivocation, and contradictions, real or apparent.

Even in 1919 and in the two following years, I was convinced and said so at the time, that the mass of the French, nothwithstanding contrary appearances, due to what I would venture to call the policy of the politicians, were really desirous of a true and lasting peace; in no place in the world was the cry ''War to end war!'' so deeply felt as among the French peasants who, on the polling day, are the real masters of France. But at the same time I felt that the mass of the French, either from excess of suffering or from want of knowledge, would have resented too strongly oversudden and radical transformations, still more when brought about by foreign pressure. This is the reason that the statesmen who in the various Supreme Councils of the time wished to force on France a too rapid revision of her judicial positions went to work the wrong way and, although sincerely

desirous of helping France by indicating her best
course, only made her defiance and bitterness worse.
I venture to say that better work was done for the
ripening of mental outlooks in France, by those who
loyally sided with her in a great number of questions, but who gave her a friendly warning when the
time had really come for her to accept a new situation. This, and no other, was the practical way at
that time to exert over French statesmen an influence all the more efficacious in that it was modest and
not self-advertising.

What holds good of the central European problem, that is the Franco-German problem, holds good
also with reference to this period, of the international life of the States of Central Europe. The same
profound contradiction surrounded their origins,
making it difficult to attain the necessary serenity in
the diplomatic negotiations which were ruling them.
Let me explain still further. The destruction of this
monstrous medieval entity, the Hapsburg monarchy,
was one of the healthiest results of the great war.
Forty millions of enslaved races, Czechs, Italians,
Croats, Serbs, Slovaks, Rumanians, ceased to bow
before a proud Teuton-Magyar minority, which itself was but the slave of two hundred aristocratic
ruling families. The addition to the European family
of those States created after the Austro-Hungarian
disruption constitutes, together with the resurrection of Poland, one of the most definite steps toward
an essential progress in European life. In fact, an
inter-European *entente* was an ideal impossible to
contemplate, so long as an old artificial State, whose
motto was *"Divide et impera,"* still existed.

A division of Europe on the basis of nationalities

is but the first step toward an associated Europe. Such was Mazzini's doctrine when, a century ago, he began his struggle against imperial Austria. A small price to pay for such a step forward, is the momentary diminution of production, such as certain gloomy economists enjoy emphasizing.

But the conflicting elements that perplexed Europe with regard to those new States originated in the fact that at the Congress, in making use of the aforesaid national principle, the treaty-makers succeeded in welding together the two habitually opposed ways of thinking. On the cradles of the new States Ariel and Caliban were, for once, of one mind. Yet the reasons for their agreement were as opposed as always. One party wanted to justify a recent war cry by the liberation of the enslaved nations. The other side desired the creation of the States with a fervor all the greater in that these States stood for them as sentries alert on guard against a future common foe. It looked like a diplomatic application of the deep psychological remark of the great Catholic theologian, St. Thomas Aquinas: "Laudable acts committed with dark intentions." There is, therefore, some excuse for the suspicions with which such creations, States that recalled to some the waning kingdoms of that overrated politician Bonaparte, were at first regarded.

It is to the honor of most of these new countries that such suspicions soon appeared vain, even to the most prejudiced. At the time of which I speak, however, some conflicting difficulties seemed very serious. I will tell you, in a future lecture, of the difficult burden that was laid upon us in the first period after the Treaty, by the atmosphere of moral contradictions which hemmed us in. But, as the chief difficulty was—and probably still is—the problem of Franco-German relations, I would rather go on now with this part of the problem. I had full opportunity of studying it at first hand, as after being Minister for Foreign Affairs at home, I was later an Ambassador in Paris.

Throughout the long-drawn years from the armistice of 1918 to the elections of May 11, 1924, which returned a radical majority to the French Parliament instead of the horizon-blue majority elected after the victory (so named from the color of the army officers uniform), throughout these years France was surrounded by an isolation all the more painful to her, in that her past history had not accustomed her to it. Notwithstanding all her deeds, her speeches, her attempts at explanations, one word was flung back at her from every quarter of the globe —militarism. Appearances were against her. But how they had come to assume such grave proportions is what I will endeavor to explain to you.

The internal collapse of Germany, and the signing of the armistice, ended four of the most terrible years in French history. A portion of the country yielded to the intoxication of victory, which is so frequently supported with less dignity than defeat. The militarist traditions of ancient France were allied to the speculations of politicians who deluded or tried to delude themselves as to the permanence of the *entente* framework, *i.e.*, of a Europe linked to France for the safeguarding of aims appearing to be essentially French. Such an *entente,* so they thought in France, should have ensured sufficient pressure being brought to bear on Germany to avert financial disaster (that fatal consequence of the War), and should have averted it by the application of that overfacile formula, which in those years was so popular in France: *"Le Boche paiera!"* ("It is for the Boche to pay"). But so clear and logical is the French mind that, even then, it perceived the fictitiousness of the plan. Hence resulted those efforts to strengthen and fortify their victory at all points, which the rest of the world mistook for aggressive militarism but which in reality were only impulses of self-defense.

First came the expedition into Cilicia, which swallowed up milliards of francs, and which was cut short, with a remarkable political courage, by a sobered France. Next, the artificial exaggeration of the mandate in Syria. Last, the help given to Kolchak's enterprises and to the mad adventures of Denikin. All of these, which were, no matter whether appropriate or not, only gestures of self-defense, were mistaken by Europe for a dangerous imperialism.

Fortunately for the real and lasting welfare of France, all in turn were checked. In Cilicia, France risked compromising her relations with Turkey, and had to retire under Turkish military attacks, to avoid the alternative of war. In Syria the mandate she had attempted to enforce by an overcentralized system of administration, solely in order to assure for herself a military contingent in possible dangers to come, had to be rectified and toned down in view of ever increasing hostility. Statistics show how far this hostility went: French imports to Syria were, toward 1922, diminished by over 30 per cent while those of Italy were doubled. The Russian enterprises ended, we all know how disastrously. As always hap-

pens in such cases, they achieved the following results, antithetical only in appearance: (1) the hatred
of the Soviet; (2) the resentment of the Czarist elements who complained of having received inade-
quate help; (3) a certain moral strengthening of the
Soviet régime in Russia, where it appeared to many
as a national régime menaced from outside. May I
add that, for having easily prophesied such results I
was, at the time, looked upon as tainted with Bolshe-
vistic plague.

Last, but not least, came the policy of violence
against beaten Germany. This policy outwardly appeared to have the whole-hearted support of French
public opinion. In Europe very rare exceptions, I
have told you before, maintained the contrary. In
France the man in the street accepted the policy of
territorial occupation, believing that Germany did
not mean to pay, and that it was necessary *"lui mettre la main au collet,"* to use a once famous Briand
phrase. But when the French masses were at last
convinced that Germany was prepared to pay the
reasonable figure to which the claim was eventually
reduced, and this occurred with the German acceptance of the Dawes plan, the Nationalists immediately found themselves isolated. At the end of 1926
M. Poincaré came into power again; but, from the
point of view of German hatred, what a changed
Poincaré! Germany had begun to pay and the
French people would no more hear of "Eternal Germany," as an enemy always to be hated and mis-
trusted, but, to quote the new Poincaré formula, of
the "two Germanies."

Having lived in France as Ambassador, and having since frequently returned to that country; famil-

iar, as I have endeavored to be, with those provincial and rural circles with which the frequenter of none but aristocratic and intellectual sets fails to reckon, I think I am able to state the real condition of the French mind after the unhappy episodes of the Ruhr. *After* those episodes, I say. Since, *before* they occurred, that great mass, so falsely represented by journalism and in particular by Paris literary journalism, had some instinctive mistrust for the Ruhr experiment. "But," they said, "supposing that the thing *did* come off! Don't let's interfere."

One is forced to believe that certain mistakes, and certain tests, must be undergone by nations. So it was perhaps with the Ruhr adventure. But I maintain that the shrewd bulk of the French peasantry, whose vote accounts for so much more than any nationalistic gossip in Paris salons, had already admitted to itself that it would not do for France to keep her troops on German soil up till the last possible minute permitted by the clauses of the treaty. France's nervous fears of Germany's military resurrection, fears which disguised themselves at first, as we have seen, in warlike and imperialistic trappings, were so alien to the best of French traditions, that in the end the country blushed for them. Hence ensued the general and sincere acceptance in France of the new Locarno policy: even though, as happens after the tempest, cross currents and storm eddies would seem, sometimes, to indicate the contrary.

I would go further yet. The ingrained common sense of the French, who, despite their revolutions remain one of the happy conservative nations, made them realize that the addition to the German Government, in January, 1927, of many Nationalists was

no real menace to France. The most lasting concessions are ever those given by an enemy. It is Poincaré's last ministry of the *Union nationale* that has
given a new force to the policy of conciliation begun
in 1924; and the same thing will probably happen in
Germany. The French understood this, and knew
that Hindenburg would be to a Germany bereft of
the Hohenzollern, what the Orleanist Thiers was to
the French Republic in 1871. I may without indiscre-
tion repeat the words spoken to me a few weeks ago
by one of the most representative German Junkers:
"We were wrong to put Hindenburg at the head of
the Reich. With that great wooden statue we have
sealed the grave from which the Hohenzollern will
never rise again." Not that excursions and alarms
between France and Germany are done with—far
from it! The moderate French views which I have
shown to you in their intimate reality have not yet
the appearance of being universal, as practically
they are, afraid as the French still seem to be of attacks from those who pretend to embody a superior
patriotism.

In Germany, on the other hand, some mysterious
forces within the State must still be reckoned with.
In both nations, a vague danger is always pending
that some sincere fanatics, or some newspapers in
pay of less sincere material interests, may imperil a
growing *entente* by acts of violence, or by incidents
artificially inflated.

The more we think of the problem, the more, it
seems to me, we must realize that the interests of
European peace and of a Franco-German *détente,* so
essential to that peace, can best be served, and
regrettable incidents and disillusionments best be

averted, in one way only, by going slowly. No sensational changes; no problems solved by one single concession; at any rate, no imagining or trying to make believe that such concessions could miraculously wipe out from the book of history whole pages of grudges, of fears, of misunderstandings. Simpler aims are, for practical purposes, sounder and surer; and all efforts should be directed at preparing a radical evolution of outlook, such as we believe to be near at hand. Of course we all wish diplomatic harmony and industrial *entente* for the two great countries. But it is still more to be wished that the rational and clear current of French thought, and the dynamic force of the German soul may cease to be, intellectually and morally, two worlds opposed.

The real feud between France and Germany has its deepest cause in their tremendous mental divergency. But Goethe, who saw it, also believed in the possibility of the gulf being spanned over. What the greatest of modern Germans hoped, we may hope.

II

POLAND AND GERMANY

IF, after having spoken of Franco-German relations, I pass at once to the relations between Germany and Poland, and to the incidental episodes which troubled those relations in the years immediately following the Versailles Treaty, it is, as you well know, because the Polish policy often seemed inspired by Paris or, at any rate, by feelings and apprehensions analogous to those of the French.

The Treaty of Versailles, besides returning Posnania to Poland, together with the so-called corridor extending to Danzig, and transforming Danzig into a free city, arranged for plebiscites to decide whether Upper Silesia and the territories of Marienwerder and Allenstein should belong to Germany or to Poland. Three electoral campaigns and three plebiscites had to be prepared. It would have taken less than that to upset the relations even between two countries on the best of terms.

The Poles are sometimes accused of a feminine want of logic. But it must be admitted that Dmowski, who with Paderewski represented Poland at the Peace Conference, was at least logical in recognizing that it was difficult and dangerous alike to cut Prussia in two by the insertion of the corridor, and an estranged Danzig; only, the remedy he proposed to eliminate that danger was simply this: to annex East Prussia itself to Poland. Probably Emmanuel Kant had not been born in vain at Königsberg some two centuries before, and none of the great Allies dared to ignore the intensely German character of this part of Prussia; the logical proposals of Dmowski were recognized as too logical to be accepted. In justice to the Polish politicians we might, however, recall the fact that Frederick II was inspired by the same "logical" reasons when, on the eve of the first partition of Poland, he wrote to his Minister in St. Petersburg: "Danzig in herself means nothing to me, but she cuts my possessions in half, and so she must be made Prussian."

Perhaps the corridor was the most dangerous gift that any fairy godmother at Versailles could have placed in a cradle. It appeared then to more than one of us that it would have been wiser to allow to Poland a sea-outlet at Memel, through some sort of union between Poland and Lithuania, which, *at that time,* it would have been easy to create.

But one can understand the reasons, the hatreds, the illusions, which, coming from certain quarters, impelled the creation of the corridor. In any case, if the corridor were to create a terrible problem, whose solution lay presumably in a far future, the three plebiscites were there, on the spot, involving with their struggles an immediate state of tension. There was this rather paradoxical result, that the very favors bestowed on Poland created serious difficulties for her in the form in which they were given, just in the first days of her independent life, either by provoking against her a poisonous press campaign, or by alarming economic interests involved in the decisions of the plebiscites.

That it had been hoped through the two plebiscites in Marienwerder and Allenstein to diminish German

territory, indicates to what point illusions or hatred
misled men's minds. The immense majority of the
population was German in the two regions. That was
not enough. The very day after a terrible war those
peoples were asked to choose between a country
where military adventures with Soviet Russia were
feared, or a country in which the treaty had sup-
pressed military service. There were many cases of
Poles in both regions voting for Germany, in order
to escape military service. The plebiscites in fact
surpassed German hopes. They were the first cold
douche which ought to have sobered the extreme
French nationalists; and, indeed, they made in
France a deep impression. At Marienwerder, in fact,
94 per cent voted for Germany, and in Allenstein 97
per cent, although the population of German nationality in both regions, great as it really was, was not
so overwhelming.

The Inter-Allied Plebiscitary Commission was
presided over at Marienwerder by the Italians, and
at Allenstein by the English. At Allenstein the Polish minority was smaller than at Marienwerder, yet
it was the Italian administration at Marienwerder
which Polish criticism, as lively as ill founded, accused of favoritism toward the German element.

The question of the plebiscite, and of the division
of Upper Silesia, created such a long and important
European controversy, that it would be quite super-
fluous to retrace its phases for you, who are thor-
oughly familiar with this period. I will only recall in
a few words the origin of the problem. In the first
draft of the treaty, Upper Silesia had been awarded
to Poland, because the majority of Silesians were
Poles. Their nationality had been recognized by the

official German documents which, before the War, had acknowledged more than a million Poles, without counting the Masurians who are also Slavs, as against 800,000 Germans, including military garrisons and functionaries. Germany protested in Paris that the Poles in Upper Silesia were as loyal German subjects as those of Teutonic blood, and that the Silesian coal was a vital necessity for her to continue with her industries and to pay the reparations. Lloyd George, who had already left far behind him the electoral program of December 11, 1918 ("hang the Kaiser, squeeze the Germans till the pips squeak," etc.), became the champion of the German cause in Upper Silesia. Hot discussion ensued; recourse was had to a plebiscite. So the plebiscite was held, resulting, in round figures, in 707,000 votes for Germany and 479,000 for Poland. You all remember that the proportion of votes given differed widely according to districts, some of which were practically unanimous for Germany and some for Poland.

Mr. Lloyd George was aware that I was always ready to support any line of action conducive to the pacification of Europe. The London Cabinet, therefore, exerted strong pressure on the Roman Cabinet for the joint formation of a majority which would have established the line of division essentially favorable to German industrial claims. At the same time, and this was a petty and annoying side of the question, Italy received from both German and Polish sources tempting proposals with regard to the future supply of coal in the case of a favorable Italian decision. I was seriously compelled to make it clear that such offers could not, at the moment, be honorably forwarded.

I must confess that the recollection of the Spa Conference (in the summer of 1920) had left with me the impression of a British, and especially a Lloyd-Georgian, policy which was rather prejudiced against Poland. The Allied ministers had come together in the famous Belgian watering place to settle the question of reparations, when their whole attention was diverted by Bolshevik military threats against Poland. Lloyd George suggested the necessity of an armistice on terms which would have seemed very hard to Poland, since by them her army would have been compelled to retire before the Red troops. It was in vain that I tried to obtain more favorable terms for the Poles. According to information in my possession, it was far from certain that Poland would be beaten. But Sir Horace Rumbold, the British Minister in Warsaw, assured his Government that the Poles might be considered as doomed. Indeed, he left Warsaw with the whole of the diplomatic corps, with the exception of the Italian Minister, Tommasini. For his part, M. Millerand (the Prime Minister who had represented France at Spa) deeply desired to help Poland, but stronger than this desire was his distaste for any sort of contact with the Bolsheviks, and he remained practically aloof. The Polish Minister, Grabski, had to accept the measures proposed by Mr. Lloyd George, which I had vainly tried to soften for Poland. A few days later, that happened which I had deemed possible. The Poles were victorious beneath the walls of Warsaw. Poland's desperate courage had found an invaluable help in General Weygand's strategical advice. At the end of August the Russians were in flight.

It was at the time of the Russian advance that
Germany and the Soviet Government established a
series of more or less verbal understandings with
each other, for which we in the West have only a few
fragments of evidence. What leaked out left me with
the impression that, in case of a Polish defeat at
Warsaw, an organized revolt was ready to spread in
Upper Silesia in the summer of 1920, which would
have been much graver than Korfanty's actual out-
bursts after the plebiscite. Halfway through August,
the entire Austro-German press announced, in a *soi-
disant* official bulletin, the capture of Warsaw by the
Bolsheviks. Instantly, at Kattowitz and in other
towns of Upper Silesia, a simultaneous revolt broke
out against the Poles and against the Franco-Italo-
British troops.

Count Oberndorf, the German representative at
Warsaw, returned thither from Berlin, on the eve of
what seemed to him the inevitable fall of the Polish
capital, and handed to the Polish Government a note,
whose subject was the dangers to which the Russian
advance was exposing those German populations
which had been delivered over to Poland by the
Treaty of Versailles. This note could have only one
practical aim, that of paving the way for an eventual
German occupation, if the Russian advance into Polish territory should be completed, a German occupation which even France would have had to condone
in order to ward off the Red peril. It may be added
that such an occupation had probably already received Russian sanction. Such an event had been
foreshadowed at the time of the Russian advance on
Poland, when the Russians signalized their entry
into each village by founding a Soviet there, except

in Soldau, the only town of the corridor to be occupied by them. There, the administration of the town was entrusted to German residents, and no Soviet was created. We may ask whether Russia had pledged herself to such a course of action by some secret understanding with Germany. Every hypothesis is permissible. We may even have come very close to assisting at a fourth partition of Poland, with the probable acquiescence of all Western Europe, if thereby a Bolshevik advance could have been checked.

But in dealing with history, it is futile to reconstruct possibilities, such as Pascal's speculations on the length of Cleopatra's nose. Enough for us here to note that both parties in Upper Silesia were effectively prepared for violent action. Why did violence break out on the Polish side only, by means of the armed bands and organizations under Korfanty's orders? We must, in justice, admit that the Polish disillusionment caused by the fact that Poland had a minority in the plebiscite was not in itself enough to let loose a revolt. Another occurrence provoked it.

The three Allied Commissioners representing France, Italy, and Great Britain in Upper Silesia had not managed to agree directly after the plebiscite on a formula to be submitted to the Allied governments. According to the treaty, this should have been done. General Le Rond, the French Commissioner wished, in spite of the plebiscite, to give all to Poland; the British Commissioner, Colonel Percival, wanted all for Germany, notwithstanding the formal decisions of the treaty concerning the application of the plebiscite. Then, without instructions from their governments, the Italian and the British

Commissioners thought it best to take it upon themselves to formulate the proposal of delimitation
which had been decreed by the Treaty of Versailles.
The Englishman gave up the idea of handing over
everything to Germany, the Italian admitted that
Germany must have the industrial zone, and Poland
the non-industrial.

What would have been the result of this division
in accordance with the plebiscite which, according to
the treaty, was to decide the line of demarcation in
Upper Silesia? We have here one of the most typical
cases of collective postwar blindness. Even today,
Germany persists in regarding the loss of part of
Upper Silesia not only as a material and moral loss,
which would be quite natural on her part, but as a
flagrant injustice, violating the clauses of the treaty
in order to harm Germany.

Now, what did the treaty say on this subject?
Simply as follows, in Art. 88:

> Germany hereby renounces in favour of Poland all rights
> and title over the *portion* of Upper Silesia lying beyond the
> frontier line fixed by the Principal Allied and Associated
> Powers as the result of the plebiscite.

And how, according to the treaty, was that formally
imposed division to be arranged? This was decided
by Paragraph 5 of the Annex to Art. 88:

> On the conclusion of the voting, the number of votes cast
> in each commune will be communicated by the Commission
> to the Principal Allied and Associated Powers, with a full
> report as to the taking of the vote and a recommendation as
> to the line which ought to be adopted as the frontier of Ger-
> many *in* Upper Silesia. In this recommendation regard will

be paid to the wishes of the inhabitants as shown by the vote. . . .

Now, by carrying out the plan of the two Commissioners, Poland would only have received 20 per cent of the population and 25 per cent of the communes, whereas the plebiscite—the basis of division as laid down by the treaty—had shown that 40 per cent of the population and 45 per cent of the communes wished to be Polish.

The Commissioners' proposal was regarded by the leaders of the Polish movement in Upper Silesia as a proof that the majority of the Powers, Great Britain and Italy, were definitely pledged to a formula disregarding the results of the plebiscite. They, therefore, thought that force alone could help them, and the insurrectionary movement broke out. General Le Rond had already left for France, which proved to me that he knew what was coming, and, as President of the Inter-Allied Commission, did not wish to have to suppress in that capacity a revolt which had his sympathy. As a Frenchman he probably shared the current French illusion that, once the Silesian mineral resources had been taken away from Germany, the latter would in the future be unable to create such a mighty arsenal as heretofore.

The revolt broke out at the time when we were in London for a Supreme Council, to discuss reparations and the Eastern question. On the way home from the Council, stopping in Paris for a few hours, I spoke of Poland with M. Briand. I told him that the Poles should instantly cut short a movement which had already cost the lives of some twenty Italian soldiers, victims to duty;[1] and that, if this were done, I should continue to favor an equitable application of the plebiscite. M. Briand then showed me telegrams informing him that the French had also sustained losses, and he appeared to appreciate my suggestion that the contents should be made public, so as to show that more than one Allied contingent had suffered; but, once I had left for Rome, he, for psychological reasons, kept silent.

In order to demonstrate that I could not permit further disorders and fresh Italian casualties, I recalled the Italian Minister to Warsaw, Tommasini, a valued diplomat whose book on Poland is a standard work. I also insisted upon the dismissal of the Polish Under-Secretary for Foreign Affairs, Pilz, who in an interview with a French journalist had declared that the Italian losses were due to the obstinacy with which our troops had tried to disarm the insurgents. The fact in itself was quite honorable for Italy, but a high Polish official should have spoken in a different tone on such a subject. Meanwhile, Pilsudski at Warsaw expressed his sorrow for the Italian casualties, and admitted that the Italian contingent had done their duty nobly. Korfanty himself expressed regret, and gratitude, toward Italy, large indemnities were allocated, and the incident closed.

After these events, Lord Curzon asked my personal opinion as to how the division of Poland should have been effected after the plebiscite. I then formulated a series of proposals which were discussed

---

[1] It was because of these Italian casualties that two years later, being Ambassador in Paris, I vetoed the granting of an Italian decoration to General Le Rond.

throughout Europe as "the Sforza line."[2] Such a line never really existed. I studied on the one hand the results of the plebiscite, and on the other the configuration of the territory, and, far from drawing up one of those vague formulae which are the last resort of diplomacy, I, on the contrary, showed the practical results which would actually be achieved on the spot. More than a "Sforza line," it was the exclusion of all other lines for which, arguing from my premises, no valid excuse could be found.

To my satisfaction, the Giolitti-Sforza Cabinet resigned in the summer of 1921. The Allies having failed to agree, the League of Nations was charged with finding a solution for the Polish problem. I quote the exact text of the decisions of the League of Nations Council on October 12, 1921, in which it declared that it would "assign to each State a number of electors not differing appreciably from the total number of votes given in its favor, and which would, at the same time, as far as possible equalize and reduce the minorities." So, by carrying out the principle which had always been mine, the same results as mine were at last unavoidably reached. No other course remained open to the League of Nations but to retrace "the Sforza line."

I must admit that, although temperamentally indifferent (too much so, perhaps) to outside opinion, I was amused two months later by an encounter on the Riviera with one of the most eminent members of the Council, who, being not without humor, confided to me: "Your line has been a nuisance to us! German propaganda had so stirred up public opinion against it that, while we wanted to do justice to

[2] See Document I, p. 99.

the claims of nationality, and interfere as little as possible with the industrial life of the country, we had at the same time to appear to strike out a new line for ourselves, a Geneva discovery. Our secretaries worked again and again on studies and classifications, but, from wherever they started out, they always had to come back to the troublesome Sforza line."

Although many of you are doubtless as cognizant of the matter as myself, it was necessary to recall to your memory this episode of Upper Silesia, which took up two years of European polemics, and is probably not yet done with, because we may draw from it some thoughts worth retaining.

The reasons which dictated my conduct belonged to three different groups. First, a general consideration: duty impelled us, as we have just now seen, honestly to apply the clauses of the treaty once the plebiscite had taken place. It was imperative that neither of the two sides should have serious cause to feel wronged. The offers which we received from both to secure our help, offers frequently renewed to myself, foolish and indiscreet as they were, might have had the result of forcing on us the strictest application of the clauses of the treaty. A second consideration was dictated to me by the thought of our most sacred traditions. Was it possible for an Italian, conscious of his country's tragic history, to exclusively accept a thesis grounded on such reasoning as this? "Every industrial region must go over to the country on which it economically depends, for the good of economic production throughout Europe." It was against such materialistic reasonings that Italy was reconstituted in 1860, after four centuries of for-

eign invasion, on the strength of one essential principle, that of nationality. Never, and nowhere, would
it be possible for her to go against that principle. An
Italian could not forget that the same train of reasoning as that which was invoked by Germany for Upper
Silesia was, in the Great War, employed against us
by the Central Empires in their propaganda, namely,
that Trieste was more useful as an Austrian port;
that the Trentino completed satisfactorily the economic region of the Austrian Alps; that its vine-
yards and its orchards would only be useless to
Italy. Yet Battisti, the member to the Austrian
Reichsrath for Trent, forgot, small Trentino land-
holder that he was, that his apples would fetch a
higher price in Vienna than in Rome, when he gave
up his life that his dead body (he was hanged in
Trent) might consecrate the Italian character of his
native region.

A third reason also was in my mind, though I must
confess that events do not so far appear to have
justified it. I continue, however, to believe that much
truth lay behind it. Let us admit at the outset that
the Polish Government has not been fortunate in its
administration of that portion of Upper Silesia al-
lotted to it by the League of Nations. The elections of
November 14, 1926, do not show a sensible increase
of Polish adherents since the plebiscite of 1921, and
this although German functionaries of every order
have been replaced by Poles. These elections even
show, on the eastern borders of the Reich, a most important frontier-zone from the industrial point of
view, that the German or pro-German minority is
now higher than the former forty per cent of the
plebiscite, in spite of the German officials' departure.

The Polish-German diplomatic tension has increased the local difficulties of an administration bound to be inferior to that of Germany. In one sense, German propaganda now has a greater force of argument than before, since it can prove this bit of lost territory (once supported by German capital and brains) to be losing annually some of its riches and some of its prosperity under Polish domination. Propaganda can also make use of the high price of living, lowness of salaries, and unemployment dole.

But when we were about to hand over this territory to Poland, I felt entitled to think that, with a little mutual good will, Upper Silesia might come to be a link between the two States; in fact, a collaboration on the basis of common economic solidarity seemed necessary. When I enlarged on this theme to those in authority in Poland, they appeared to take in my ideas. One, who, for fear of exposing him to the overheated nationalistic rancor of his countrymen, shall be nameless, even went so afar as to say to me, "Yes, I see that between us Poles and Germans it is absolutely necessary to arrive at a sort of common exploitation." This did not come to pass, yet there was no reason why it should not have been, should not yet be, some day. If the new tendency of Franco-German policy is confirmed, a policy of collaboration between Germany and Poland may be fraught with fewer difficulties. Indeed, it would be useless to have concluded a pact on the Rhine, if seeds of violence still germinated upon the banks of the Vistula.

The resurrection of Poland constitutes one of the brightest moral lights in the Versailles Treaty. But Poland, through no fault of her own, still suffers from having become a great country too rapidly, and through an external miracle. True wisdom would for the present, at any rate, lead her to emulate the French statesman who, when a friend questioned him after the Terror, "What have you been doing all this time?" replied, with naked simplicity, "I have lived."

A terrible problem certainly divides Germany and Poland, not that of Upper Silesia, but the corridor. Yet we must remember in this connection that the best work for European peace is not always done by those who angrily denounce injustice, demanding that the treaties which caused it be formally revised. No, in the interest of peace, it would be sufficient to interpret the treaties and slowly find out new applications and compromises. As for the spirit in which this work should be approached, we may find examples even in nineteenth century Germany. Germany ensured her power, her prosperity, and her future at two stages of the Bismarckian period. First, when the Chancellor, in spite of King William's wishes, declined to take an inch of Austrian territory after the Austrian defeat of 1866, and so gained a prolonged alliance with that country. Again, when the same Chancellor, content to have continental supremacy, refused to hear a word about the empire of the seas. The unhappy neurasthenic who drove him out, and who was himself his own Chancellor, did not possess the wisest of political gifts, I mean the sense of limitation, hence his downfall.

We may sometimes wonder whether the last of the Hohenzollerns and the rhetorical "iron fist" and "dry powder" Germany he impersonated and, we believe, falsified, are not going to take a strange revenge on some of Germany's neighbors. This revenge might be the revival among those neighbors of that militaristic overbearingness and nationalistic conceit which brought upon her, through the fault of her blind leaders, so hard a visitation.

III

THE SUCCESSOR STATES OF AUSTRIA-HUNGARY

LORD SALISBURY used to say that the chief responsibility for all the silly things said or thought about
the gravity of Anglo-Russian relations lay with the
geographical atlas, which gave the impression to the
casual observer that the Russian bear was waiting
round the corner, scarcely concealed behind some
mountains, for the chance to stride across them and
to hurl himself upon India.

It would not surprise me if a like simplicity of
conception had helped to create that nostalgia for a
lost Austria-Hungary which it has been the fashion latterly to cherish in Europe. Men of mature age
had, many of them, grown used to seeing on the map
a vast, unicolored blot, joining itself to those others
which symbolized Russia, Germany, and Italy. To
the south lay lesser barred stains of color, Serbia,
Rumania, and others, and from their direction used
to come rumors of war and uprisings. Small wonder
if, watching the barred stains spread northward,
amid the complications of a postwar period, a sharp-
ened regret was felt for the appearance of solidity
which had formerly been presented by the Hapsburg
monarchy.

Other psychological elements, more serious if
equally illusory, have gone to form, all over Europe,
a kind of posthumous benevolence toward Austria-
Hungary. In the first place, there is the Church of
Rome. The Vatican knew well enough how little true

Christianity, or even Catholicity, lay behind the outward pietism of the monarchy, of the aristocracy, of the bureaucratic government. Austria-Hungary remained, however, the single great state whose sovereign, annually, on the first Sunday in June, followed bareheaded the solemn procession of Corpus Christi, as it wound through the streets of his capital for hour after hour. The Roman Church was aware that so much external homage must frequently be paid for by her in a servile obedience to Austrian governmental interests, in painful compromises in Albania and the East, where even her own claims sometimes had to yield before those which the Ambassador of Francis Joseph imperiously imposed. But these unfortunate incidents occurred in secret; the external prestige was all the Church's. And, above all, that Church disliked the successors. It was felt in the Vatican that John Huss, burnt alive by order of the Council of Constance, had suffered also as promoter of the national Czech spirit, as the spiritual hero of Bohemia. The entire work of de-nationalizing Bohemia had been accomplished, under the Empress Maria Theresa and her son Joseph II, by the creation of a new Austrian aristocracy recruited from among adventurers of Flanders, France, and Italy, who had hired themselves out to the Empire, and who received their new Czech fiefs on one condition, fidelity to Vienna and suppression of all efforts at a Slav resurrection. In this work the fief-holders had the constant support of the Catholic bishops. These are inflictions and sufferings not easily forgotten. When, in fact, the memory of the national hero, Huss, was celebrated at Prague two years ago, the ceremonies were not long in assuming an anti-Catholic appearance.

In France also there was a strong Austrophile tradition; not among the people, conscious of no such bond, but in the aristocratic salons as well as in the studies of certain diplomats. It was more from snobbery than from any other motive; it helped them to play at politics, not to pursue politics them-selves. The last Empress of Austria had been born a Bourbon princess, of the Italianized branch of the old dukedom of Parma, indeed, but none the less a descendant of Louis XIV. One of her brothers had established himself in France, where he had married a bride of the French aristocracy, and where he was displaying a keen French patriotism. It was this young gentleman, the "dear Sixtus," to whom Charles, Emperor of Austria, turned in 1917 to try and conclude a separate peace. It was proposed to France that she should betray her treaties with Italy. Painful uncertainty ensued, but the sentiment of French honor was stronger than diplomatic calculations, and the offer was rejected.[1] The cunning Austrian proposal had provoked painful uncertainty. This was among certain ranks of French diplomacy, touched by temptation in one of its oldest and dearest traditions; but even those diplomats, to their honor be it said, refrained from entering a sphere where the word, that is, the dignity, of France would have lost so much.

Of what did those traditions and temptations consist? Of this: that French diplomacy sometimes pays the penalty for having an almost too finished historical and political culture. I have often fancied that

[1] See Document X, p. 125.

the pigeonholes of the Quai d'Orsay must each contain, ready to hand, a copy of the Peace of Westpha-
lia, the ideas of which, inspired as they were by the
period corresponding to the end of the Thirty Years'
War (1648), still seem to have some part in direct-
ing the trend of French political thought. The West-
phalian idea was to keep the Germanic race broken
up in fragments; what a temptation, then to make
use of an Austro-Hungarian Monarchy which might
eventually have absorbed Bavaria and other countries of the Reich, on the strength of its Catholic
characteristics. As frequently happens, even the
great newspapers gave the impression of sharing
these illusions, blind terrors and pleasant lies being
the alternate menu of the upper classes' daily intellectual food. A most unique and certainly the most
courageous exception was the old *Journal des Débats*
which strongly denounced the vain hopes of playing
Austria against Germany and, by doing so, served
the interests and the honor of France as well as the
Italian national cause.

I have sometimes frankly discussed these retro-
spective but still ticklish questions, thanks to a
friendship wherein numerous actions had rendered
graceful phrases unnecessary on my part, with those
among French statesmen who had a secret weakness
for Austria at the bottom of their hearts. One of
them was Paul Deschanel, whom I saw frequently
after his resignation as President of the Republic.

"Leaving aside," I used to tell them, "the rights
of nationality, the feelings of Italy, the consequent
alienation of Italian, Serb, and Rumanian sympathies, apart from all this, you would have based your
chief support on artificial and unsound construc-

tions. Think, for example, of one who, for all his nervous lack of equilibrium, was no common mind, the
Archduke Franz Ferdinand, heir to the Hapsburg
throne, who was assassinated at Serajevo, what was
the aim and object of his 'Trialism'? The only way
out for Austria, but also her complete abdication as
a Germanic power."

These doubts were comprehended; yet, in politics
hatred is stronger than friendship, and the hatred
felt for Germany was a blinding force in some cases.
Hence it may be concluded (in parentheses) that a
sane policy of Franco-German *rapprochement,* far
from injuring French intimacy with the Successor
States of Austria, as certain polemists claim, would
only ensure it more firmly.

In view of this persistence of certain longings and
regrets in Europe, even if these were psychological
rather than political, and considering also the pres-
ence in Switzerland of the ex-Emperor Charles,
claimant to the Hungarian throne, it was natural
that the Successor States should have become conscious of common ties which presently developed
into the Little Entente.

The first diplomatic act marking their union was
the Czecho-Yugoslav Convention signed in Belgrade
on August 14, 1920, by M. Benes, Czechoslovak Minister for Foreign Affairs, and M. Ninchich, Yugoslav
Minister of Commerce, then in charge of the Ministry for Foreign Affairs in the absence of its titular
head, M. Trumbich. Three men, they were, who had
too long suffered personally under Austria not to
agree quickly on a common defensive action in the
event of attack from Hungary, prepared to take back
Charles of Hapsburg as her king. The convention,

indeed, only envisaged an unprovoked attack on the part of Hungary, but those who signed the convention knew, even then, that the links which they were then forging were destined to have a wider diplomatic outcome.

Immediately afterward, in Belgrade itself, M. Benes made a declaration to a press representative which showed clearly the trend of the new pact. Let me quote it verbatim, convinced as I am that semiofficial words, so long as they are authentic, contain more of the breath of life than correct and proper diplomatic statements.

"We have no intention whatever," said the Czech Minister, "of launching into external adventures, but our wish, once our internal consolidation is accomplished, is to profit therefrom to collaborate with the *Entente* for a definite restoration of general peace. This was the object of my journey. We want a policy of wide horizons aiming at the stabilization of Central Europe. Such a policy is advantageous to the Allies, since it reinforces their authority. We are equally glad to prove to those who regret the dismemberment of Austria, or dream of a Confederation of the Danube, that Central and South-eastern Europe can perfectly well consolidate itself by means of a direct *Entente* between the principal successors to the Dual Monarchy. We have one especial aim besides, which is to bring home to the Magyars that they must learn wisdom, and cease to be a hotbed of unrest. Here also, we are guided, not by selfish national interests, but by those of European peace which we are taking in hand."

European diplomacy gave different and opposite interpretations to the creation of the Czecho-Yugoslav group, attributing it, according to individual tastes or suspicions, to French or Italian influence. In Poland, for example, the treaty was believed to have been concluded under my influence, I being then Minister for Foreign Affairs, which justified a certain attitude of reserve for fear of displeasing Paris. In point of fact (to the highest possible credit of two ministers whose countries were not among the Great Powers) these ministers had acted independently of all foreign influence, their conduct being dictated solely by the political and historical aspect of the situation, as viewed by their consciences and their patriotism. Later, I will speak of the only sense in which I may have influenced the signing of the convention, by the conversations which I had had a month before (July, 1920,) at Spa, during the Inter-Allied Conference, with M. Trumbich, Minister for Foreign Affairs of the Serb-Croat-Slovene Kingdom.

But, keeping for the moment only to those external events which dictated to the two countries such measures of precaution as they took, let us recall the following: Hungary had never ceased to exploit the fact that fairly important Magyar minorities, saturated with an admirable and fervent patriotism, had been absorbed into the new neighboring States; more than 300,000 Magyars, indeed, had passed into Yugoslavia, more than half a million into Rumania, and 600,000 into Czechoslovakia. A clandestine propaganda emanating from Budapest kept up the unrest among these minorities. It must be admitted that the Successor States would have been better advised to try to reduce the minorities to the lowest figure compatible with sure and logical frontiers, instead of pandering to land-hunger, and to a spirit of vengeance directed at the haughty race which had held them in submission for centuries. This secret Magyar propaganda took the most varied forms; for instance, a violent outbreak at Sabolitza in April, 1920, was fomented by Magyar nationalist elements, joined for that end to communist elements. Certain other associations, such as "The Awakening Magyars," while they did not stoop to complicity with communists, yet maintained a continuous stream of agents and spies, coming and going all about the ancient territory of St. Stephen's crown.

This campaign for the reconquest of old frontiers went hand in hand with that of the monarchists. Impossible that it should have been otherwise. On leaving Austria, after his defeat in Italy, the Emperor Charles had merely signed a paper declaring his royal powers in Hungary to be suspended. This was not an act of abdication. Moreover, to be valid according to Magyar law, it should have been countersigned by the Hungarian Prime Minister and then registered by Parliament. These formalities had not been carried out, and they were a living thing in Hungary, where by an old medieval tradition it was still held that the material crown placed on the King's head at his coronation was an integral necessity for the completion of his royal right. According to the Hungarian legitimists, it followed that, Charles not having signed the peace treaties, his sovereignty extended over those territories which the Rumanians, the Yugoslavs, and the Czechs held by a might which was not fully right.

In the summer of 1920, those currents of French feeling to which I have already alluded as intensely favorable to the reconstitution of Hapsburg power

were strengthened by two elements. First, by the
fear of Bolshevism, which led to the belief that a
feudal and monarchical Hungary might be a sure
rampart against it, a rather arbitrary conception,
since the Serbian peasants, for example, all of them
democrats and all small landowners, are assuredly
at least as safe from any germ of Bolshevism as
some of the Hungarian agricultural proletariat. Sec-
ondly, the fact that at the beginning of Horthy's
régime, English and French capitalists had invested
large sums in important Hungarian business, and
that, consequently, as well as through the newspapers which they controlled, they were in process of
rekindling ancient Magyar sympathies. Already,
through these foreign interests, the headquarters of
the Inter-Allied Danube Commission had been fixed
in Budapest, instead of Galatz in Rumania, or Pres-
burg in Czechoslavakia.

Against these and other symptoms of British and
French indifference the Czech and Yugoslav statesmen, at the time could count only on my open sympathy for any course of action opposed to the dangers of any sort of Hapsburg restoration.

I will be brief at this point, wishing to speak as
little as possible of myself and only when it is un-
avoidable to make clear the links of the events.

At the Spa Conference, I had particularly earnest
talks with the Yugoslav Minister for Foreign Affairs, M. Trumbich. You all know that the Adriatic
question had, up till then, entailed a lengthy and bitter series of polemics. Now, our conversations held
a new note. I told M. Trumbich, whom I had known
in Corfu during the War, and of whose anti-Aus-
trian feeling I was absolutely sure, that I was not

unaware of all the difficulties entailed by past events
upon my present course of action; but that I was
prepared to brave any unpopularity in the lasting
interests of Italy; that the Government of Belgrade
was confronted, in the Giolitti-Sforza Cabinet, by a
strong Government ready to act, to take decisions,
and to assume responsibilities; but that I could not
accept the territorial bases agreed to by my prede-
cessors, according to which the frontier-line passed
within ten kilometres of Trieste. Those *pourparlers*
I should consider as not having occurred. The Belgrade Government must realize that I should have
proved inflexible as to the necessity of a complete
Alpine frontier, with the "Massif" of Nevoso in
Italian hands; but that, on the other hand, I should
have treated with Belgrade in a novel spirit of collaboration and understanding; and that our diplomatic union might have proved valuable against all
danger of an artificial Austro-Hungarian recon-
struction coming from no matter what source. Belgrade understood this novel language, which paved
the way for the Treaty of Rapallo, signed by us on
November 12, 1920, ensuring to Italy the complete
Alpine frontier.

To this precedent I alluded, in mentioning previously that the Czech and Yugoslav statesmen knew
that my full sympathy could be gained for their joint
labors.

This work of theirs was continued at Rapallo, for,
on the same day as the two delegations signed the
treaty which ensured to Italy the Alps, the whole of
Istria, Zara, the islands of Cherso, Lussin, and other
lesser isles, and also ensured the Italian character of
Fiume joined to Italian territory, with a privileged

rule for Italians living in Dalmatia, the three Italian plenipotentiaries and the three Yugoslav plenipotentiaries put their signatures to an anti-Hapsburg convention.[2]

I quote from this convention the following articles:

1. The two Governments pledge themselves jointly to take all political measures calculated to prevent the restoration of the House of Hapsburg either to the throne of Austria or that of Hungary;
2. The two Governments pledge themselves to afford, each to the other, such diplomatic assistance as is most suitable to attain the above aim;
3. The two Governments pledge themselves to mark all activities directed against their reciprocal safety, whether coming from Austrian or from Hungarian territory, and to that end they will maintain the closest possible contact with each other.

Another article added:

The Italian Government, which has learned with satisfaction the understanding established between the Serb-Croat-Slovene Government and the Czechoslovak Government (exclusively with the same object as the present Agreement), and the Serb-Croat-Slovene Government, will bring this convention to the knowledge of the Czechoslovak Government.

As you see, this convention was conceived in the same spirit as that at Belgrade three months earlier between the Czechs and the Serbs. Only the hypothesis of a war was no more in question. From the moment when Italy entered the lists, such an hy-

[2] See Document II, p. 101.

pothesis became a practical impossibility. Hungary would never have ventured upon war. Successive Italian Governments have renewed more or less analogous engagements in new forms since then. It could not have been otherwise.

Although there was at that time, in Italy, an attempt by certain parties and newspapers to show that the Little Entente, in addition to various other more or less imaginary misdeeds, contained the embryo danger of a federated union to reconstitute Austria-Hungary in a new shape, the fact was, and still remains, overevident: (1) that the Successor States had too great a love for their newly regained independence to sink it in any kind of federation which might be obnoxious to Italy; (2) that a Hungarian state of some twenty million inhabitants, including a Croatia detached from Yugoslavia and gravitating perforce toward the Upper Adriatic to menace the Italian character of Fiume, would have constituted for Italy a more trying alternative to a Yugoslav state, the center of which is a Serbia ever more drawn toward the Lower Adriatic and the Aegean, a deadly enemy, moreover, of old Hapsburg institutions, whose disappearance was, for Italy, the sovereign gain of the War.

M. Benes, one of the most intelligent ministrants to European peace, came to see me in Rome at the beginning of February, 1921. We had on this occasion an exchange of letters.[3] Those instruments brought Czechslovakia into the sphere of action of the anti-Hapsburg convention.

At the end of March, 1921, there followed Charles

[3] See Document III, p. 102.

of Hapsburg's first attempt to return to Hungary. You are too familiar with the diplomatic history of these last few years for me to enlarge upon the details of this lamentable venture. I merely wish to testify, from my own accurate recollections of the moment, that the great Magyar peasant majority was adamant to the ex-King's appeal. He was surrounded only by the loyalty, sometimes sincere and admirable, but sometimes assumed for material interests, of certain great families, who had all to gain by consolidating their ancient feudal and patrimonial privileges through the King's return. The Cabinets of Rome, Belgrade, and Prague acted in perfect accord, and with great rapidity. Admiral Horthy's government wisely realized that Charles must be sent back, if fatal consequences were to be averted; and the ex-King returned to Switzerland.

A certain small incident now occurred. Prague and Belgrade were convinced that Charles would certainly repeat his attempt; and they wished to take steps at Berne with regard to him. The Swiss Government being extremely sensitive, and justly so, concerning its right of asylum, I was asked to interpret, in a courteous manner, the feelings shared by us all, including myself, in this matter. The Federal Government sent me the reply that it would demand of Charles his word of honor not to make a second attempt. I answered that he would give his word, but that on the first occasion he would be obliged by his entourage to break it. This remark caused some scandalized feelings among the republicans of the Federal Council, yet a few months later they were forced to see that I was right.

A conference of the Successor States of Austria

now assembled at the Chigi Palace in Rome, under my presidency, and in an atmosphere of trust and collaboration. Those economic questions which existed between our respective countries were to be discussed at it. "We will prove to all Europe," I declared in my opening address, "and prove it with the matchless eloquence of facts, that in existing society it is impossible to conceive an economic state of real well-being not indissolubly joined to the well-being of our neighbors." These are overevident truths today; in 1921 they were suspiciously criticised.

A new link of the Little Entente was forged on August 23, 1921, and on the fifth of June following, by two treaties which, in the same spirit as their forerunners, allied Rumania with Czechoslovakia and with Yugoslavia, respectively. M. Take Jonescu, the lamented Rumanian statesman, had previously informed me of the shaping of these treaties, asking my advice and my assent, which, of course, were given with cordiality and sincerity.

Another treaty had been signed in March, 1921, but one which did not precisely fit into the framework of the Little Entente. I refer to the Polish-Rumanian Treaty guaranteeing reciprocal help in the event of attack by Russia. Those conversant with popular feeling in Serbia and in Czechoslovakia know how impossible it would be for either country to enter upon a treaty hostile to Russia, whether under Bolshevik rule or no.

Poland, meanwhile, was not opposed to a system of relations based upon the wish to suppress all attempts at restoring the former State of Austria-Hungary more or less to her former condition, but Poland wished to remain out of it. Prince Sapieha, then Polish Minister for Foreign Affairs, thought, mistakenly, that such a system was displeasing to Paris. Not until the question of Upper Silesia became a burning one, and the Poles began to be anxious as to the application of the plebiscite in that region, did Prince Sapieha make advances to me, in the direction of the Polish adhesion to the anti-Hapsburg convention. But these exchanges of ideas only took serious and concrete form when M. Skirmunt succeeded Prince Sapieha. Skirmunt, who had formerly been accredited Minister to Rome, had there witnessed my line of action, and convinced himself that Polish interests were also involved: particularly, that there lay one of Poland's means of maintaining really intimate relations with Italy. M. Skirmunt, a Lithuanian-Pole full of good sense, understood also that it was useless to continue a kind of political coquetry with Hungary solely in order to annoy Prague, and that it was better worth while to be on good terms with his near neighbors.

Changes caused by parliamentary crises prevented M. Skirmunt from carrying on his work. An understanding achieved by him with Czechoslovakia was not well received by Polish public opinion. This is not astonishing. The Poles gave proof of their strong chivalrous sentiments, inherited from the past, when they repelled the Bolshevik invasion in the summer of 1920; but political good judgment, independent of likings and antipathies, comes to a nation only after much practice in public life. And Poland had only just emerged from a long period of slavery.

The Cabinets of the Successor States diverged from each other at various other small points. A few genuine enthusiasts, and a greater number of adventurers who prowled round Hertenstein in Switzerland, convinced the unfortunate Charles that the moment had returned to try his fate. In spite of the word which he had pledged, he launched himself upon the new venture, even as I had predicted to the Federal Council. The rest belongs to history. The states of the Little Entente regained the most complete unity in the face of danger; even Poland backing up the Czechoslovakian "démarches" in Budapest. The Great Powers, by their intervention, and Charles, through his weakness of temperament, together rendered Czecho-Yugoslav mobilization unnecessary. After an interval of some hundred hours, at which he played at Kingship, this unhappy descendant of a race which had produced so many decisive and able characters, was shipped aboard the British monitor *Glow-worm,* and began the first stages of his journey to Madeira, where he died on April 1, 1922.

You know what was the evil motto of his house—"Divide et impera." A house guilty of the declaration of war on Serbia, that declaration which unchained the European War, needs not to be accused of further crimes; their conscience bears a sufficient burden. Yet we should not forget how the House of Hapsburg had always endeavored to keep alive the divisions of Eastern Europe, in order to further its own power. May we, then, hope that, now the principal source of jealousies and divisions having disappeared, a more peaceful future is opening for Eastern Europe than she has ever known?

For my part, I unhesitatingly incline to optimism, even to the certainty that, in a more or less remote future, Bulgaria may be drawn to the other Yugo-slav countries in a kind of Federal Union, although I know that the dweller amongst ancient rancors in Macedonia, Serbia, and Bulgaria may think my vision Utopian. Optimism is justifiable only if these States are going to be let alone; if they are allowed to be themselves, and nothing else. If some among them should at any time allow themselves to become again catspaws for the secret quarrels and jealousies which bigger States dare not openly avow, then, ah! there indeed we may tremble lest the sterile and gory history of the East be reopened once more. There is, however, ground for confidence in the knowledge that the old Hapsburg Austria is dead, the domineering Austria of whom Joseph de Maistre, who had studied her from the two opposing observation posts of Petersburg and Turin, used to say that she was always harmful, but even more to those who trusted in her than to her enemies.

It is not hate that makes me adopt the judgment issued a century ago by the great Savoyard political thinker. I know only too well that, sometimes even unconsciously, we in Europe are apt, out of hereditary feelings, to think in the way of hate. It is our curse; it is the penalty we have to pay for so many centuries of history.

Here in America you are rightly proud and thankful for your greatness, your prosperity, your immense future possibilities. There is one thing you ought to be even more thankful for—that you have no hates. It is a characteristic of yours which strikes me every day and adds, in my spirit, to the glorious peace of the country where I am now living.

The Emperors who ruled from the Hofburg in

Vienna fifty million men with ten different lan-
guages, ten opposite traditions, knew that their only
safety lay in the constant jealousies among all these
races: Croats against Hungarians, Hungarians
against Austrians, Slovenes against Italians, and so
on. It was not enough; Austrian diplomacy was always at work for mischief between, let us say, Serbia
and Bulgaria, between Bulgaria and Rumania. Bal-
kan nations at peace with each other might have
meant progress for them; they might have become
hopeful centers of irredentist dreams for the Austrian subjects of similar nationalities.

An artificial source of hates between fifty millions
of Europeans has therefore disappeared with the
disappearance of the Hapsburg monarchy, which
was indeed nothing else than a sterile oligarchy of
courtiers and bureaucrats, with no spiritual message
for the world.

Is it now much better? Probably not. Some new in-
justices have probably replaced some of the old ones,
new resentments have added to old hatreds. But the
great fact remains, where artificial and diplomatic
Austria was standing, stand now living nations.
Each of them had and may have again a part in Europe's progress: Hungary, which was so long our
valiant rampart against an aggressive Moslem East,
Czechoslovakia, which gave with Huss a great mar-
tyr to religious freedom; Yugoslavia, where West
and East meet under the same language; Rumania,
with her peaceful and sad folklore. Each of these
nations may commit blunders; but, like England,
France, Germany and Italy, they are living entities;
they are the real permanent material out of which a
newly organized Europe will some day emerge.

IV

THE ALLIED POWERS AND TURKEY

Did I not tell you, at the beginning of these lectures, that it was difficult to find an historical period more full of paradoxical contradictions than the postwar period? I do not think, for instance, that it would be an exaggeration to affirm that the armistice signed in the roadstead of Mudros on October 30, 1918, on board the warship *Superb,* between the delegates of the Sublime Porte and the British Admiral Calthorpe, found the two recent enemies in complete agreement, on at least two points: the feverish haste of its conclusion, and the desire to create, as speedily as possible, a new situation which would make it impossible for General Franchet d'Esperey, the French Commander-in-Chief of the Army of the East (composed of French, English, Italian, and Serbian forces), to march on Constantinople and there instal himself as master. The fact is that the Armistice of Mudros imposed upon the Turks neither precise nor serious conditions as to disarmament, disbanding of troops, nor penalties against, or the removal of, certain heads of the party "Union and Progress."

If the haste and slackness of the Armistice of Mudros proves that the most pressing consideration there was to avert the development of a situation in which some other Allied force would hold the military preponderance, one may also draw from it the conclusion that, at that particular time, the end of the War, what afterward became so determined an English policy, viz.: the destruction of the Turkish Empire, was far from being intended. This will only surprise systematic minds of French or German formation, that is to say, reasoning and logical minds which never can take into account that the rapid changes which, on our continent, are so often attributed to the perfidy of Albion are in reality due to no other cause than to the rough-and-ready empiricism and improvisation which are part of the British political make-up.

Some days after the armistice, England, France, and Italy decided to entrust the guarding of their interests in Turkey to three High Commissioners. The Englishman was Admiral Calthorpe (a signatory of the Armistice of Mudros), the French, Admiral Amet (who commanded the French squadron in the Levant), the Italian, myself.

In reality, at that moment of the apparent destruction of all Turkish authority, and pending the negotiations of the Big Four in Paris, our task was rather that of governors. We had at our orders the squadrons in the Bosphorus and the military contingents on shore. We organized an administration, a guardianship of order, and the revival of the Allies' banking, educational, religious, and other institutions which had been destroyed or closed during the years of war. The three High Commissioners held their meetings once a week in their respective embassies by turns, each time under the presidency of the master of the house. The Serbian, Greek, Rumanian, and other representatives, following each other to Constantinople, presented themselves before us as before a Supreme Local Council and our

administration was carried on without too much national rivalry; our harmony and loyalty were constant. At first my two colleagues were inclined to
think that I was too lenient in my dealings with the
Turks; that I showed, perhaps, a little too much regard for the conquered Sultan; that, personally, I
was too cordial toward the former grand viziers and
other personages of the Empire, who little by little
came out of their hiding places; that I did not suffi-
ciently ignore the Sublime Porte. I am sure that during the first weeks of that winter (1918-1919) the
two admirals, in the bottom of their hearts, must
have put down this weakness of mine to my unfortunate quality of civilian. But they were men full of
good sense. Little by little they felt that I was guided
by very serious reasons: the conviction that Turkey
was far from dead, that she was only temporarily
down and that, if we pulled the rope too tight, she
would escape from our hands; we might remain masters of Constantinople, but we should be masters of
a wonderful empty house; the active forces of Turkey would retire deeper into Asia, out of our reach,
and that, once there, they would turn against us.

This situation and these anticipations I had, from
the very first, communicated to my Government. I
informed it that I could only serve my country by
acting on these ideas, and that I would interpret its
silence as implying approval of my line of policy. I
could not expect much more than silent approval, for
my conception of the potential situation of the Turkish people excluded those projects of Asiatic partition that were being entertained in Paris, in which it
was sought to interest the Italian Government.

The Sultan, weak and uncertain, violent in little

things and cowardly in serious, was the typical descendant and head of a dynasty that is condemned
and whose rôle is ended. He had chosen as grand
vizier, Ferid Damad Pasha, who, as the title
"Damad" indicates had married one of the Sultan's
sisters, Princess Alidé. Ferid had studied at Oxford;
he was, to all outward appearance, a very successful
copy of an English gentleman. In reality, nothing
and no one in official Turkey showed the slightest
sign of life or strength. Those who, in London, tried
to persuade Mr. Lloyd George and Lord Curzon that
they could, in the future, do anything they liked in
Turkey had reason to believe they were right.

Now and again I saw, and did not conceal the fact,
the few men who afterward made up the ruling class
at Angora, among them, Mustafa Kemal who, as the
hero of the defense of the Dardanelles, was already
popular amongst the Turks. I felt that these men
were speaking the truth when they declared their
ability to maintain their independence in Asia,
whither they were already inclined to withdraw.
When, therefore, on May 12, 1919, Admiral Calthorpe invited his French and Italian colleagues to
the English embassy to communicate to them instructions from the Conference of Paris with regard
to the occupation of Smyrna by the Greeks, I, for my
part, was convinced that the affairs of the *Entente*
would take a very bad turn in Turkey. But our
instructions were categorical and nothing could be
done. The landing was what it was bound to be, what,
at the meeting of the High Commissioners, I had
expressed the fear that it would be, a fightless yet
bloody operation, whence issued, wounded to death,
the party whose violence could appear to have been

successful only to those who could not see through appearances. Greece was doomed from the day she planted her flag in Smyrna.

On the landing of the Greeks, the Turkish troops had at once withdrawn into their barracks. They acted so by the orders of the grand vizier who, not from treachery but from weakness and well-meaning, had sent emissaries to Smyrna advising resignation and giving assurances that the Greek occupation would be only temporary. Moreover, there were not then in Smyrna any of those *fedais* (the sacrificed) who became, at a later date, fanatics to the death in the Turkish national cause.

Who, then, fired from the barracks the first shot which let loose the massacre? My informers assured me at the time that it was a Greek *agent provocateur*. It is probable; not, certainly in consequence of political instructions from Athens, but owing to the folly of some Greek commander who wanted to fight an easy "battle" and win a still more easy "victory." However it may be, if up to then there had been hopes of finding a solution equally acceptable to everyone, after the Smyrna landing it was too late. Mistakes in politics, as in moral life, beget mistakes.

The Sublime Porte had previously been guilty of the imprudence of sending Mustafa Kemal away from Constantinople by giving him a command in Asia. He was near Samsun when the news of the occupation of Smyrna reached him. He summoned the people together and made them a speech which moved them to tears. An English officer, who was in the district, dispatched a telegram to Constantinople demanding the immediate recall of the young general. The Sublime Porte was invited to issue such an

order; with the forms that it had inherited from
Byzantium, Mustafa was cautiously invited to come
to Stamboul only to discuss the general situation.

He displayed a trait still more Byzantine when
friends, or prospective friends, from the Porte itself, warned him urgently that the summons was going to be dispatched. He who had not yet decided to
break with the capital, it may be from a patriotic
sentiment, set out on a tour of inspection toward
Erzerum and thus avoided the necessity of ignoring
an order from the Sultan, an order that, so to speak,
never reached him.

I am telling you these facts, which have probably
never before been made public, because you will
draw from them this conclusion: that with a certain
amount of moral courage the situation might still
have been saved.

Why was it not? Partly, I am afraid, because I
was the only High Commissioner who told his capital and Paris that it was not only desirable, but imperative, to conclude a peace with Turkey satisfac-
tory to all sides; that Turkish satisfaction would be
the best guarantee of advantages that we should
have acquired all the same; that if we asked for too
much we would run the risk of a complete loss of our
position. If my colleagues at Constantinople did not
express themselves with equal decision, it was not
because they were far from sharing my convictions,
but only that, being members of fighting services,
they were, as such, imbued with the psychosis of war
and hesitated to state clearly what they could not
fail to perceive in the depths of their consciences.

It was in Paris at the Peace Conference that
everything conspired to confuse men's minds. The

French, engrossed as they were by their situation on the Rhine, were not inclined to oppose too plainly the English on a part of the chessboard less vital to themselves. It was the same with the Italians, preoccupied exclusively in their turn, with the Adriatic question. The English—the English were Mr. Lloyd George and Lord Curzon.

Nobody has been more struck than I by the late Prime Minister's rare qualities of intuition and rapidity of action. During the War in his quarrels with the generals he was always right, as when he wished to break the enemy mass by driving into Austria with a gigantic Anglo-Italian effort, whilst some of the British field marshals had no other tactics than this: in attack, to find out the enemy in his strongest position and hurl themselves upon him; in defense, to stop and resist heroically and die.

But West is West and East is East. And Mr. Lloyd George, in the West, had learned to know by himself. Moreover, he, a "frock," as Sir Henry Wilson mockingly called the civilians, was suspicious of the general views of the "brass-hats." In the East what he believed to be the military truth was put before him by another "frock," Mr. Venizelos. Mr. Venizelos is also a very remarkable man, and had powerful excuses for having miscalculated the forces at work in the East. He dreamed a great dream, the "megala idea" which had consoled so many generations of Greeks during centuries of slavery and misery. He hoped to realize it with the help of England, who seemed to him all-powerful.

The fatal error was committed, and, since no one wished to acknowledge it, the situation throughout all Turkey, beginning at Constantinople, grew worse. An English Intelligence Service, composed of specialist officers, took over all the political and police control. The blunders which these specialists committed contributed not a little to shake Occidental prestige. Allow me by way of example to recapitulate to you one of the finest feats of what was designated the Inter-Allied Police, but which, in fact, was British.

One morning it was reported that a great conspiracy was about to destroy the Allies. The Commander-in-Chief of the Allied Army of Occupation was warned that a vast conspiracy had been formed to raise a revolution in Constantinople to assassinate himself and several other officers. He furnished the Turkish authorities with a list of the supposed guilty parties, whose arrest he demanded within one week, failing which he would be compelled to take vigorous measures against the population. The list presented by General Harrington to the Ottoman Minister of War contained twenty-eight names, of which eleven belonged to Turkish politicians then residing in Angora, whilst the other seventeen were insufficiently described and completely unknown persons. Only by their first names and by their places of origin did the English police describe the authors of the redoubtable conspiracy. There was no question of arresting the parties in Angora; but how discover, in Constantinople, Ali of Yalova or Mehmed of Trebizond?

The Turks were not at a loss in so small a matter. They congratulated General Harrington on having fortunately escaped so great a danger, and themselves on their capital having been saved from so frightful a crime, promising to do all in their power to secure the arrest of those guilty ones. The few names of politicians inscribed on the famous list threw sufficient light on its origin. The commander of the Allied forces had, of course, acted in absolute good faith, but the Orientals who had invented and denounced the plot simply wanted to get the men then in office into difficulties in order to step into their places. Nevertheless, rather than cast a doubt on the reality of the plot, or even on the existence of the accused, the Ottoman authorities said to themselves that there were in Constantinople a dozen Alis and Mehmeds who were not worth the rope to hang them. Eight were found at once, and hanged. General Harrington rendered public tribute to the loyalty of the Turkish Government, and withdrew his threats. This was merely comic, except for the hanged ones, but what followed was both tragic and irreparable.

On March 16, 1920, General Milne, commanding the English forces, occupied all the important positions in the capital, the Ministry of War, the telegraph- and post-offices, and ordered the arrest of several dozen senators and deputies. A state of siege was proclaimed. A few days later, the Sheik-ul-Islam issued the *fetva* proclaiming the Nationalists at Angora to be rebels and excluding them from the Moslem community.

The reply was not long delayed. On April 23, 1920, the National Assembly in Angora inaugurated its labors with solemn prayer, and elected a Grand Council to which it entrusted the carrying out of its decisions. Mustafa Kemal was the soul and real head of this Council. A few days later the Grand Council transformed itself into a Provisional Cabi-

net, the word "Provisional" being employed merely
to show that the Nationalists had no intention of giving up Constantinople. The Minister of Foreign
Affairs was Bekir Sami Bey, a Mussulman of the
Caucasus, who, the year following, represented the
Government of Angora at the Supreme Council in
London. The politics of Angora became decisively
xenophobic, embracing in its hatred both English and
French. It was the consequence of the facts already
known at Angora which were later to result in the
stillborn Treaty of Sèvres of which you know the
sense. The Italians alone were not ill treated, the effect of the attitude of good will that I had adopted
from the beginning.

You are acquainted with the sequence of events.
Mustafa first of all raised armed bands, and behind
them organized a solid army. The stronger he grew
the more the Turks turned to him. The very officials
of the Sublime Porte longed in their hearts for his
triumph. To the Turks the end was henceforth plain.
It was only a question of time. One point only remained uncertain, variable. This was the decision of
the Allies, who in April, 1920, at San Remo had
ended by accepting the hard English terms of peace.

On the eve of San Remo, in March, Lord Curzon
said, "The effective strength of Kemal has been
overestimated, he is not as important a factor as
some assert," and, by this general phrase "some"
he referred to the man who has now the honor of
speaking to you.

Moreover, in June, after San Remo, Mr. Lloyd
George declared in a great speech that Greece only
was capable of "taking the place" of the Ottoman
Government. At Hythe, toward the end of June, Mr.

Lloyd George had a meeting with the French Premier Millerand. Mr. Venizelos offered England, whose military situation in Turkey had finished by becoming dangerous, the complete collaboration of all the Greek forces. The plan drawn up by Mr. Venizelos provided for the swift march toward the interior of Anatolia, of a well-equipped army of 90,-000 Greeks, who would cut all Kemal's lateral communications and force him to retire into the interior where his forces would be dissolved. The French prime minister was resigned rather than disposed to accept the project, being pushed thereto by general diplomatic considerations and by the preoccupations which the Turks were causing him on the Cilician-Syrian frontier. But the consent of Italy was necessary; and for the purpose of obtaining it a meeting of the Supreme Council was held at Boulogne-sur-Mer immediately afterward. I had just taken the direction of the Italian foreign policy, and went there to represent Italy.

Apropos of the projected Hellenic invasion of Anatolia, I declared formally that it would be a very grave mistake, and that if it were desired to redouble the life and strength of Turkish militarism and nationalism, that would certainly be the best line to take to ensure it.

A month afterward, we met again for the conference at Spa (July, 1920). Mr. Venizelos presented himself there, for the last time, to urge his proposal before the Supreme Council, and to have his way. The Council was composed of Lloyd George, Millerand, and myself.

Venizelos set forth his reasons for being certain of success. I was the only one who replied, opposing his argument by showing the danger that Greece would run, and I finished my reply with these very words: "My only regret is that the attitude of Italy should be attributed to want of sympathy or even distrust toward Greece. I feel myself, on the contrary, inspired by sentiments of deep concern for her true interests. No peace is good that is not a peace tolerable to both sides. The Greeks in gaining too much risk losing everything. I am quite sure that in this hall there is at least one person who feels the deep sincerity of my words, and that person is Mr. Venizelos."

When I had finished speaking I felt that rare pleasure that one never experiences from the applause of crowds and parliaments. I looked at Mr. Venizelos and saw from the expression of his face, always so open and of such quick intelligence, that he had appreciated the deep sincerity of my words, and that, if only for a moment, the impression had come upon him that some day they might prove too true. But the die was cast already, and you all know in what a tragic fashion it ended for Greece two years later.

The conference which met in London in February, 1921, should have opened the eyes of the most confident. What did we see there? The delegation of imperial Turkey, of the Sublime Porte, was headed by a venerable man respected by all, Tewfik Pasha, who had been grand vizier many times. The delegation from Angora was also there, headed by their Minister of Foreign Affairs, Bekir Sami Bey. The British Government refused to receive the latter by itself, for fear of thus according Angora a sort of official recognition. To the astounded eyes of the Occiden-

tals there appeared one morning, in perfect harmony, and sitting on the same bench, the two delegations who were supposed to hate each other, as those
engaged in civil strife know how to hate. In our eyes,
in English eyes, the venerable Tewfik Pasha was the
head of all these Turks, but he asserted his position
of chief solely in order to yield the word to Bekir
Sami Bey, who was the only spokesman on the side
of the Turks, of either Stamboul or Angora.

I then tried to use my influence over Bekir to make
him adopt a moderate attitude. I was fortunate
enough to succeed. He showed himself more willing
than the Greeks to place himself in the hands of an
impartial arbitrator. An arbitration was decided
upon. It was to take place after an enquiry. Now this
was already a point gained, and this was why I first
started the idea, feeling sure that Mr. Lloyd George
would end by adopting it, since he had, with ample
reason, less sympathy with the new Greek premier,
Mr. Calogeropulos, than with his predecessor, and
was beginning to feel less confidence in the future of
Greece.

When Great Britain, France, and Italy proposed
an enquiry, it was in effect to acknowledge that the
authors of the Treaty of Sèvres had been ill informed, and that it was necessary to begin again
from the beginning. This deprived Angora of all reason for intransigence and opened a future way for
all possibilities.

Thanks to the intelligent understanding of Bekir,
I also cleared the way of the tripartite agreement
which pledged France, Great Britain, and Italy to
guarantee the latter a special sphere of economic in-

fluence in Anatolia. Bekir signed with me a new treaty, spontaneously recognizing, under certain clauses, a series of Italian privileges in the same zone.[1] An act of free will was thus substituted for a convention imposed upon the Turks from outside without consulting them.

So it seemed still possible to secure soon a tolerable peace. But it was nothing of the kind. Three months later the Oriental situation again grew worse. The Greeks had rejected the Commission of Enquiry, and decided to resort to arms.

You know all about this unhappy adventure. The Greeks, beaten at first, succeeded in the summer of 1921 in occupying Afium-Karahissar and Kutaja. The front held firm for one year, but in August, 1922, the reconstituted Turkish army destroyed the Greek front and occupied Smyrna. King Constantine lost his throne. Great Britain, France, and Italy interposed between Turks and Greeks. The result of four years of blunders, illusions, and excessive pretensions was the Armistice of Mudania on October 11, 1922, by which Europe was obliged to consent to the reëntry into Constantinople of the Nationalists and to that of the Turkish Government into Eastern Thrace; in short, the complete return of the Turk into Europe. The Treaty of Lausanne only served to accentuate the end of all European privilege.

Chance willed that I should take part in the negotiations that preceded the Armistice of Mudania. I was no longer Minister of Foreign Affairs, but Ambassador in Paris, and as the negotiations took place in Paris, whither Lord Curzon had come, it was we

[1] See Document IV, p. 104.

three, Curzon, Poincaré, and myself, who had to deal with the question.

I shall never forget the sad confession that Lord Curzon, with tears in his eyes, made to me one afternoon in a room on the Quai d'Orsay. Proud as he was, he owned, to his credit, honestly, that he had made a mistake, and that it was the man he was addressing who, for all his apparent anti-nationalistic slackness, had best tried to guard the interests of the West. Such regrets, however, are useless in politics, altogether meritorious though they may be in moral psychology.

What then was wrong during the post-Versailles period, with the Oriental policy of England, at other times and on other occasions so generous and far-sighted? If we endeavor to answer this question, we shall at the same time draw from these souvenirs a lasting moral. For governments of great empires it is more necessary than for small countries to judge apparent successes and apparent checks with the sobering background of history. As life is continuous and men have memories and expectations, the leaders who think of an immediate success are rarely doing service to that august continuity which is the history of a great country. It was perhaps possible to destroy the Turks; although the attempt did not succeed. It was impossible to believe that, by so doing, a mortal blow would be dealt to the Moslem World, and to its cohesion and spirit of resistance. This spirit of resistance is merely the Mussulman defensive: a defensive provoked by fear. The essential thing is to remove this fear.

Can it still be done? Yes! it can, because the East still wants the West more than we think. I say it for the Near East as well as for the Far East. But the problem of establishing, let us say of reëstablishing, European influence in the East cannot be—will never be—a simple problem of force.

V

A EUROPEAN MICROCOSM

OF late years it has been the fashion to lament that
the treaties of 1919 "balkanized" Europe, that is,
that they served to cut it up into far too many small
states whose very existence harbors and multiplies
the seeds of war. From hearing these criticisms, one
might be led to ask oneself whether the Great War
had really been provoked by, say Denmark or Switzerland, or rather by the preconceived intention of
one of the greatest European states, Austria-Hungary. No; the lesser nations, so long as each of them
forms a real and well-defined national entity, will be
among the truest sureties for peace in the Europe of
tomorrow. And this, not only because small nations
have a deeper concern for peace than is ever the case
with the greater ones (since, in war, they have all
to lose by being invariably trampled upon by the
giants), but also because the salvation and the future
unity of Europe are nearer the hearts of the small
than of the great peoples. It is the little states which
cling to the League of Nations with, at times, an
almost embarrassing affection. Moreover, even a lesser nationality, if it has succeeded in keeping its life
and literature intact, is one of the flames of human
thought. By what right, therefore, should one wish
that flame extinguished? Finland, which has fought
for her existence under the Russian Terror, has a
finer message for humanity than, let us say, the old
bureaucratic Austria-Hungary, which was formed

by the compression of ten nationalities, with not one single idea of her own.

So, I do not think it will be a waste of your time if I examine with you the efforts toward international life made by the Baltic States since their independence.

You are all too familiar with European political problems for me to squander your time in generalities. You know that, in the course of the nineteenth century, which was the era of new-found nationalities, a swift awakening befell even the little Baltic nations, each differing so profoundly in race and language from its powerful German and Russian neighbors. Finland, Esthonia, Latvia, only awaited the right moment for asserting their own life; the moment came, with the Great War.

At the beginning of 1920 I was struck with the strong and frank tone of an Esthonian diplomatic document which came under my notice at the Italian Ministry of Foreign Affairs. The document reads as follows: "It is said in Europe that, if Russia had not crumbled, the Baltic States could never have been born, and that if Russia were to resume her place in the concert of the Powers, the fate of some of us would be at stake. We venture to think that we owe our own independence not solely to the fall of Russia. That empire seemed a mighty one; but it contained the germ of disruption in its violent policy toward the allogeneous nationalities. Events hastened the hour of our deliverance; but in any case it would have struck, some day. A living nation cannot be killed; justice cannot with impunity be tampered with." This optimistic language was no bluff, for a simple reason: because it was sincere. Similar speech and feeling were to be met at Riga, the capital of Latvia, and at Helsingfors, the capital of Finland. Subsequent events showed that these small States had the will to live, and were alive. It is therefore well that we should study them. History is not merely a natural phenomenon, as some sociologists would have it, but a moral phenomenon also.

The history of great territories may be paltry, once the hour of decadence has struck for a country. Inversely, there are periods when the history of small States may hold significance and interest. Indeed, it is because the Baltic States constitute a kind of microcosm, by their compactness facilitating observation, that I will ask you to study, with what may seem a tedious amount of detail, their recent history and their efforts for union. We shall thus prove that the idea of a Baltic Union, which already existed before the Baltic people won their independence, has not ceased since then to direct the international policy of those States. Such a union seemed inevitable, even apart from the interests of the new-born States, as being a continuation or a resumption of a European political tradition. That is the standing necessity to prevent the Baltic from becoming a *mare clausum* dominated by the strongest occupant of its shores. Fortunately, moreover, the call to union rang out more clearly among the Baltic States, then in the act of formation, because it was imperative to face a common danger, and simultaneously to acquire a part in European politics which corresponded to their vitality.

In the spring of 1917, the events in Russia had aroused great expectations in Latvia and Esthonia, as amongst all races oppressed by Czardom.

They hoped for a large share of autonomy in the
loosened administration of the Russian State. But
the realization was soon forced upon them that the
provisional Russian Government lent itself unwill-
ingly to such a lessening of central authority. Moreover, the Russian Liberals were undecided ideolo-
gists. After them, Kerenski was—Kerenski. So, when
in November, 1917, the Bolsheviki seized hold of
power, and when disbanded Russian troops joined
themselves to Bolshevik forces in order to pillage the
country, the Latvians, who in spite of schemings
and promises made by nobles of Germanic origin,
had maintained their moral independence, resolved,
together with the Esthonians further north, to break
all ties which still held them to Russia, and to de-
clare their entire independence. This proclamation
was made in Esthonia on September 24, 1918; in Latvia, where greater hindrances were caused by the
intrigues of German feudalists, who owned a large
part of the Latvian soil, a similar declaration came
only on November 18.

The successful occupation of Esthonia by German
troops deferred the organizing of national independence. Those Esthonian politicians who were able to
escape the authorities in occupation, and to avoid
imprisonment, managed to go abroad and set to
work to acquaint the Allies and neutrals with the
aspirations of their people. These first efforts at
Esthonian and Latvian independence were, with
few variants, those of other countries which broke
away from Russia. All patriots from Finland, Esthonia, Latvia, and Lithuania, who were refugees in
Stockholm, London, and Paris, met and conferred
among themselves, exchanged the longings, vows,

dreams of their races, and united their efforts to ensure for them a successful realization. It was amongst these men, without diplomatic experience, but with a great love for their countries downtrodden by the invader, that the Baltic *entente* first took shape. Each of them thought not merely of obtaining selfish advantages for his country, but rising to a loftier understanding of their collective interests, acted with the view of securing for all alike the same rights and guarantees.

At these meetings of the Baltic delegates held in London and Paris in 1918 and 1919, were discussed nothing less than the general status of northeastern Europe and the international status of the Baltic. A Swedish statesman, Branting, who later on won such deserved esteem at Geneva, did not hesitate to join them. The formation of a vast Baltic Union was even considered, the idea of which was not abandoned by some before the middle of 1920. One finds, indeed, a last vestige of it in the provisional program for the Conference of Bulduri, near Riga, of August, 1920, in which Poland, Finland, Esthonia, Latvia, and Lithuania took part, a program that contemplated, also, the participation of the Scandinavian States, Sweden, Norway, and Denmark.

The provisional rules of the conference contained, in fact, in their first article the following: ''The countries that will take part in the Conference of Baltic States as members enjoying equal rights are: Finland, Esthonia, Latvia, Lithuania, and Poland. The Scandinavian States Sweden, Norway, and Denmark may be added to the above-mentioned countries if they express the wish to take part in the Conference.''

This was not expressed and the great Baltic Union, for some time contemplated, still rests in the domain of future possibilities. When Esthonia, after a struggle of over a year waged simultaneously on two fronts, found it advisable to discuss Soviet proposals of peace, she wished to lay the foundations of a general peace between Russia and all her Baltic neighbors. She could not, even at the risk of losing precious supports, fail to take the only road that assured her safety. Waging a purely defensive war it was impossible, the country being freed and the enemy driven over the frontier, to repel the offer made to her. The Esthonian Government was, moreover, bound to avoid any appearance of getting implicated in any intervention in the internal affairs of Russia, for this would not have been understood or approved by the people, sorely tried and exhausted as they were by successive occupations of the country and their hard campaigns of liberation. Still the Esthonian Government was none the less anxious to remain closely united to its allies. Therefore, the first condition that it made with the Bolsheviki, before engaging in negotiations, was the suspension of hostilities with Finland, Latvia, and Lithuania. Moreover, at the very moment of carrying on the Esthono-Russian peace negotiations, Esthonia was represented at the Baltic Conference at Helsingfors in January, 1920, and joined Finland, Latvia, and Poland in deciding to conclude a military defensive convention.

If Esthonia was the first to sign a peace with Russia, Latvia was not long in following suit and signed the Russian peace at Riga on August 11, 1920. Finland signed hers, at Tartu, on October 14 of the same year. By these treaties Soviet Russia unreservedly recognized the independence and absolute sovereignty of the three States and renounced all rights that had been exercised by the old imperial Russia.

It was a basis of life, but very feeble; and the three States realized that it was necessary for their existence to effect the Baltic Union. This Union was to be the outcome of the Bulduri Conference, which I have already mentioned in connection with the primitive dream of a Balto-Scandinavian Union. To tell the truth, circumstances were most favorable for the success of this design. As nothing helps to unite two peoples so much as a common fear or a common hatred,—hatreds, alas, in foreign politics binding much more closely than affinities—circumstances could not do otherwise than increase the reasons in favor of union. It was, in fact, the period of the great Red push on Warsaw. The defeat of Poland would rightly have seemed to be the prologue to the loss of her smaller neighbors. On the other hand, the Secretary of State of the United States had just issued his famous note on the indivisibility of Russia, and his consequent refusal to recognize the States arising from its dismemberment, with the exception of Poland and Finland. Finland, Poland, Esthonia, Latvia, and Lithuania, taking part in this conference, found themselves, therefore, naturally disposed to find in union a strength and a guarantee of existence which was not to be found elsewhere.

The program of the conference included the conclusion of a military defensive convention, the examination of very many economic and financial questions, such as commercial exchanges, patent

rights, permanent exhibitions, the creation of a
Superior Economic Council, a common banking
policy, the unification of railway systems, etc. The
labors of the conference lasted five weeks during
which success was attained in establishing an economic convention, and a convention relative to extra-
dition and to mutual assistance in judicial matters.

Moreover, a convention creating a permanent
Court of Arbitration, to which the contracting States
engaged themselves to submit all differences arising
between them, was signed by a majority of the par-
ticipating States. Certain dispositions of it were
singularly categorical, such as, for example, those of
Article 6, which ran as follows: ''The fact of having
recourse to the Court of Arbitration entails the obligation of submitting conscientiously to its decisions.
In the event of one of the parties refusing to con-
form to this engagement, all the other Contracting
Parties pledge themselves to insist upon the carrying out of the Decree, and to compel by every means
within their power the submission of the recalcitrant
party.''

But the essential part of the program of the conference, the conclusion of a military defensive alliance, and, in fact, the realization of the Baltic Union,
remained unexecuted, by reason of the Vilna dispute
between Poland and Lithuania. The conference sepa-
rated in the hope that a speedy settlement of the dispute would render it possible soon to finish the work
begun.

On the morrow of the Bulduri meeting, the Baltic
delegations proceeded to Geneva to formulate their
request for admission into the League of Nations.
The demand of Finland was granted forthwith. The

demands of Esthonia, Latvia, and Lithuania were not acceded to for the reason that their recognition *de jure* had not been accorded by the Great Allied Powers. This was a heavy blow for Latvia and for Esthonia; but in two months time, on January 21, 1921, one of the Supreme Councils, which at that time met periodically, came together in Paris. The Baltic delegates returned to Paris, to plead their cause once more.

For my part, being then a member of the Supreme Council, I was agreeably impressed by the air of serious competency, modest but assured, of men such as Mejeroviz, the Latvian delegate, or Pusta, the Esthonian, the latter of whom was later on to develop a course of action, so meritorious and so well carried out, in the cause of the Baltic League.

When the question of recognizing these States came before the Council, an incident occurred which is curious enough to be mentioned here. M. Briand, who presided at the meeting, having begun by asking his colleagues' opinion, Lord Curzon demanded to be heard. With his solemn Victorian eloquence, which on no occasion he forgot to use, he enlarged for half an hour upon the inconvenience and unwisdom of committing ourselves definitely with regard to the Baltic States; if ever the formula of another British statesman, "wait and see," was to be used, this was really the case. One could not foresee what the future might bring in that direction; and, while expressing the best of good will toward the Baltic States, he felt it best to remain, as it were, agnostic with regard to them.

I next demanded a hearing, declaring that I could not follow the reasoning of my British colleague. It was not possible to be more Russian than the Russian Government itself; and, since that Government had recognized Latvia, Esthonia, and Georgia, and since we were concerned with races differing totally from the Russian people in language and mental outlook, it seemed to me unjust and impolitic not to accord to them such support and strengthening as the recognition *de jure* would afford. The Baltic peoples had already proved themselves worthy of their independence at a grave crisis. It was right that the Great Powers should show confidence in them.

Next I developed those political reasons counselling, in the interest of Georgia, that the recognition of that country should be deferred. M. Briand agreed with me. Lord Curzon, only partially shaken, was about to rise and reply to me, when Mr. Lloyd George arose and said: "I have listened to the opposite views of Lord Curzon and of Count Sforza. I must admit that I share our Italian colleague's point of view." The embarrassment of Lord Curzon, so sensitive in his *amour propre,* is present with me still. I tried to salve his hurt by saying that such divisions of opinion on the merit of a question, even between statesmen belonging to the same country, were the most hopeful signs of progress toward the organic unity of Europe. I am afraid I grossly exaggerated; but, in the Chinese phrase, Lord Curzon's face was saved.

Two years after the attempt of Bulduri, the Baltic States held another meeting, this time at Warsaw. It occurred in March, 1922, on the eve of the Genoa Conference. The Polish-Baltic Conference had for president Skirmunt, then Polish Minister for Foreign Affairs—a solid Lithuanian full of common sense.

Work was carried on with a cordiality expressive of a wish for understanding. A convention was, indeed, established whereby Poland, Latvia, Esthonia, and Finland undertook: (1) to acquaint each other with all treaties which any of the parties involved might conclude with another State; (2) to maintain a benevolent reciprocal neutrality and to give concerted help to any of the parties attacked, without provocation, by a fifth State.

The Finnish Government did not, however, decide to bring this treaty before its parliament. The convention, therefore, remained unratified; but its moral importance was none the less great. Moreover, their community of race and language with the Esthonians, and the proofs of cohesion given by the two neighboring republics, are constantly increasing in Finland the movement of complete solidarity.

The failure of the Geneva Protocol, a scheme so popular among the lesser states, reinduced the Baltic republics to consider the conclusion of a union among themselves. The *lacunae* of the Covenant, so clearly exposed at Geneva, the fact that a door remained opened to war after the rejection of the Protocol, urged the Baltic States afresh to ensure for each other reciprocal supplementary guarantees. A general Convention of Arbitration and of Conciliation was signed, at the conference of Polish, Finnish, Esthonian, and Latvian Ministers for Foreign Affairs, met together at Helsingfors on January 17, 1925.[1] This time, the convention was ratified by all signatories, and is actually in working order.

[1] See Document VI, p. 108.

In August, 1925, a fresh conference was prepared at Reval. M. Pusta, then the Minister for Foreign Affairs for Esthonia, had drawn up a scheme of protocol accentuating, in a happy formula, the intimacy existing between the parties in question, and fixing semiannual meetings between the Ministers for Foreign Affairs of all four countries.[2] Participation in these plans was already ensured when the meeting had to be postponed on account of the sudden death of M. Mejeroviz. Further meetings, however, confirmed the close union between Finland, Esthonia, and Latvia, with a common contact with Poland on all questions relating to the maintenance of peace. It may even be said that general feeling becomes more and more united on that subject, since M. Erich, one of the most important politicians of Finland, the country which had hitherto been the most reluctant to commit itself by the written word, has lately launched the idea of a northern Locarno.

It would be judging the situation too narrowly to object that, after so many attempts, the only written bond between the Baltic States—Lithuania being excepted on account of the Vilna question—is the General Convention of Arbitration and Conciliation signed at Helsingfors in January, 1925. Written texts go but a little way toward establishing a moral atmosphere. In fact, virtually, psychologically, the Baltic Union already exists. The truth of this will henceforth prove itself whenever these States are confronted by a problem which concerns their status. The fact of their identical interests, or, if you will, fears, will constantly impel them to a concerted and frequently unified course of action. This has already

[2] See Document VII, p. 116.

been demonstrated at every meeting of the League of Nations, where their views have never yet been divergent. The most recent proof of this is the manner in which each one is now carrying on *pourparlers* with Russia to conclude a pact of security. Not being able to establish with the Soviet Government, the collective premise for a northern Locarno, as Moscow has been willing to begin only isolated conversations with each State, Finland, Latvia, and Esthonia have thought it necessary to submit to the Russian will and have agreed to hold isolated *pourparlers* with their powerful neighbor; but, at the same time they have decided to keep each other constantly acquainted with the progress of the conversations in order to maintain an identical attitude. Russia, scorning in words, but adopting in reality the tricks of the old diplomacy, wanted to play one state against the other. Their loyal decision renders vain the Soviet Machiavellianism. The visit of the Ministers of Foreign Affairs of Finland and Latvia, last winter, to their Esthonian colleague, was intended to mark the close solidarity with which all these states intend to work together toward Russia. The decision to renew constantly such meetings will end by giving the impression of the periodical assembly of a superstate.

The very fact that no solemn, completed formula of a Baltic Union has yet been possible of achievement increases, to my mind, the feeling of a real unity. Reciprocal difficulties are not being ignored; the consciousness that much still remains to be done renders the effort toward completion greater. Every time that divergent interests make themselves felt, work proceeds gradually, by indirect stages, smoothing down by bilateral treaties such obstacles as might delay progress toward the goal. A whole network of commercial treaties has been formed between the Baltic States. Latvia and Esthonia concluded a defensive alliance on November 1, 1923.[3] The closest agreements already existed between Finland and Esthonia, countries of identical race. On her side, Latvia signed with Lithuania, on July 1, 1925, a convention which has since been renewed, and which seems to be the possible starting point for a very close economic alliance. Finally, and chiefly, Latvia and Esthonia have now established and signed their Economic and Customs Alliance.[4] The customs frontier between the two countries has ceased to exist. Last June the two Ministers of Foreign Affairs met in Reval to remove jointly all minor technical difficulties, and ensure, even in the details, the unification of the Latvian-Esthonian economic policy.

Had I not grounds for saying that it was worth our while to study what these small states are doing? Where else in our Europe, more and more divided by economic barbed wires, could we hope to hear, I do not say of such an achievement, but simply of such a scheme?

So, we are confronted with concrete and profound realizations, and we have the right to think that the Baltic Union will end by asuming a common juridical form, maybe that of a kind of Commonwealth where each State will retain its sovereign rights to the full; something analogous, though starting from

[3] See Document V, p. 105.
[4] See Document VIII, p. 118.

opposite standpoints, to the shape the British Dominions are taking.

It would seem that, in spite of their shared terror of the Russian neighbor—which fear, we must admit, is the beginning of wisdom—the Baltic States have but slowly advanced toward formal union, as if, at first, they wanted to taste, each of them, the full and young joys and responsibilities of independent existence. Only after having been completely Latvian, Esthonian, Finnish, did they, with growing conviction, close the links that bound them—links which ensure safety, but do not crush individual vitality.

You realize for what imperative European reasons we must follow the development of this Baltic microcosm in its international life. It reproduces all those causes of fear and hope, all those interests and ideals which, by reversing the magnifying-glass, we can see spread over the whole of Europe. With this difference: that in our old Europe not only are the obstacles gigantically greater, but long historical traditions of feeling and thought make our march forward so far more complicated. The dead, with us, in Europe, have almost as great a share in our political decisions as the living. It is only fair for you, here in America, when you are apt to pass a quick condemnation on our errors and our madnesses, which indeed are grave and real, to remember that our long past is like a medal with two sides. If one bears our glories and our historical creations, the other one is charged with the saddening memories of our grudges and of our rancors.

THE ROMAN CATHOLIC CHURCH AND EUROPEAN NATIONALISMS

You all know how cautious are in general the official speeches of diplomats, cautious to the point of becoming a collection of empty truisms. When on January 1 of the present year (1927), the various Diplomatic Corps presented their traditional good wishes to the Heads of States to whom they are accredited, they took the greatest care not to depart from the highly respected custom of speaking so as to say next to nothing.

Two exceptions only occurred in Europe. It is remarkable that one of these occurred in the French and the other in the German capital. Remarkable also, that the authors of these two exceptional speeches were the Nuncios of the Holy See who spoke, the one to M. Doumergue and the other to Marshal von Hindenburg, in their capacity as Doyens (deans) of the Diplomatic Corps. These two speeches are worth re-reading, even so many months after their delivery, and I certainly do not know of many analogous instances in recent diplomatic oratory. The speech of Monsignor Maglione, Nuncio in Paris, is as follows: "Monsieur le President, the Diplomatic Corps, whose interpreter I have the honor to be, are happy to offer Your Excellency, in the names of the governments they represent, and in their own, their best wishes for the new year.

"Deign to accept them. They are sincere and

heartfelt; they tell with what sympathy and satisfaction we follow the efforts put forth by France for the pacification of the peoples. We feel sure that your Government will continue this work, worthy of the traditions of your country, of its most noble soul and heart. The full confidence we already felt has been further confirmed by the projects that your Minister for Foreign Affairs announced, a little more than three months ago, to the representatives of so many nations. None can recall without emotion the discourse he then pronounced. His words, so eloquent and so profoundly felt, expressed the desire of the nations for reconciliation and that spiritual brotherhood which will enable them to heal their wounds and guide them, through wholly peaceful emulation, toward ever higher moral, economic, and social progress.

"In this beneficent work France may be assured of the active and loyal collaboration of our governments, and in particular, permit me to say so, of Him who has never ceased to plead, with the tenderness of a father and in the name of the Prince of Peace, for a disarmament of minds.

"God grant that soon, and in all truth may prove applicable to the relations which shall exist between the members of the great human family, the words of holy writ so joyfully recalled in our liturgy for the season, 'Justice and peace have kissed each other.' "

On the same morning the Papal Nuncio in Berlin expressed the good wishes of the Diplomatic Body to President von Hindenburg. Monsignor Pacelli's speech, although, perhaps, in a less buoyant tone, was in perfect analogy with that of his colleague in Paris, which gave a clear indication, if any were needed, that the two prelates spoke according to instructions from the Holy See. The particular distinction of the past year, said Monsignor Pacelli, has been the fact that it saw the entry into the League of Nations of the great country that President von Hindenburg so wisely guided. In spite of many obstacles the idea of peace and international coöperation had gained considerable ground, even though it was not yet possible to foresee the final effect of the efforts made in that direction. It was to be hoped that the seed sown would yield a rich harvest in the new year.

In his reply the President said that if, as the Nuncio had remarked, it was as yet impossible to foresee with certainty whether the efforts to achieve an understanding among the nations would have the desired success, he too was convinced that these endeavors must be continued with the greatest energy, in order that the idea that all the nations are bound by common interests might become a reality. By her participation in the international agreement concluded, Germany had, during the past year, as the Nuncio had pointed out, again placed on record her willingness to collaborate in this task.

On his side, the President of the French Republic in his reply to Monsignor Maglione took note, with particular pleasure, of the sympathy with which the work of pacification that France had traced for herself is followed throughout the world. He added: "The year just ended has awakened an immense hopefulness in the countries still bruised and bleeding from the war. Marking fresh progress on the road to the reconciliation of the nations and the settlement of differences by arbitration, it has at last seen the establishment amongst the peoples, armed against each other in so many conflicts, of a peaceful collaboration which will be, for the world, a sure gage of security, if each brings thereto sincere good will and a spirit of generous humanity, without departing from a loyal observation of international engagements.''

This final "if" seemed to some, at the time, to imply a condition put on the Franco-German *rapprochement*, or even to be a warning. It was, in fact, coming from the mouth of the head of a State, merely the bare enunciation of a plain natural necessity. To show how deep were his feelings, the French President added a sentence which, almost in the same words, was, at the same moment, pronounced by the German President. "More than ever does it appear that the prosperity of a country cannot be conceived independently of that of other countries." Simple truths, these are. But it was something that they were recognized at the same moment in Berlin and in Paris.

Apropos of this last phrase I have quoted, may I be permitted to recall a personal souvenir, solely with a view to showing that time, for all our blunders, has not passed in vain, and that even these words constituted a serious step forward from a gloomy past? In March, 1922, I presented my credentials as Ambassador to the predecessor of the present French President. My speech, which was somewhat discussed afterward and, within the limits of French extreme courtesy, criticized in French conservative circles, ventured to insist twice (I say ventured because such words were not heard in official France in 1922) on the "necessity of a common work for the moral and economic peace of Europe." This peace, I added, "could only be found in a forth-coming general *entente* of the whole of western Europe."

The President, who was then M. Millerand, assured me in his answer that he shared all my views with regard to *entente* and peace "in the world." I bowed, apparently satisfied, but felt at once that to answer "world" to my "Europe" was but a courteous way, not of denying, but of evading the problem.

The speeches of the two Nuncios, in Paris and Berlin, made a deep impression throughout Europe.

At first, in France, the essential ideas in the Nuncio's speech and in President Doumergue's answer were not so much discussed as the fact that a foreign representative had seemed to take sides in what to many still appeared to be a purely French question: namely, the direction to be given to French foreign policy. This is not so strange when one considers the proud tradition of moral independence of all outside interference which, even among the most faithful French Roman Catholics, created the Gallican spirit, once famous in the relations between the Holy See and the French kingdom. Even amongst the warmest friends of the new Locarno policy many suspected that the Vatican was aiming at something more concrete and immediate than the restoration of real peace in Europe. "Does the Vatican aim at the creation of a French parliamentary Center Party such as exists in Germany?" was the suspicious Gallican question. In short, that happened which nearly always happens in political discussions. Immediate interests, the passions of the moment, got the upper hand of farsighted views.

But time soon quieted all these polemics and, in

the case of the manifestations of the Holy See last January, history did her work rapidly. A few months have been sufficient to show that the Vatican, first criticized almost everywhere by excited minds, was, this time, inspired by a thought that soared far above and beyond the tactical interests of governments and parties.

What tempts me into taking for the subject of our last meeting the Papal thought concerning the problem of European peace, is not so much the decisions the Vatican has arrived at, important as they are, as the study of the various stages and psychological moments the Holy See went through. We have in them, if I am not mistaken, a sort of deep mirror in which are reflected the unceasing preoccupations of the Christian world, preoccupations of concern to the Vatican, which finds itself compelled to reach a synthesis concluded above political frontiers and moral barriers. Daily political preoccupations, with their ordinary compromises, make themselves felt in the Vatican as in any human place; but this synthesis, which is no less than the echoes of the human sorrows and hopes, ends by overruling minor preoccupations and fears.

We must, indeed, not forget that the Roman Church sees often clearer and farther owing to the fact that, by her very nature, she is bound, even if sometimes she seems to forget it, to disregard side issues, preoccupied as she is with handing on to a future, near or remote, that sum of ideas of which the Pontiff considers himself only the temporary and responsible guardian.

The majority of governments are harassed by claims and rancors, the immediate satisfaction of which appears to them essential; and the Locarno achievements are to be paid, sometimes, by petty concessions to Caliban, in words or deeds, whereas the Church of Rome has felt, has ended by feeling, what a terrible burden of responsibility would rest upon her doctrines if these were used for the purpose of unchaining or risking another war. She has, at the same time, perceived what immense consequences for or against Catholicism might depend one day upon her loyalty to or indifference toward the present intense need of reconciliation between the members of the distracted European family. She has understood that this need does not proceed from a state of mind changing like a fashion, but from an optimistic obligation, a sadly optimistic obligation, I would dare to say, for henceforth the nations must come to an understanding, or perish, must agree together by force if not by love. And taking into account that this need had already found concrete, if somewhat mediocre expression at Geneva, the Church has drawn therefrom the inference that this great human movement, which may take even a sort of religious form in the case of its purest adepts, must not develop outside the Church and almost against her. Former bias against the League of Nations is quickly forgotten at the Vatican. The solemn pronouncements of the Church, even in the period of armed peace that preceded and made inevitable the Great War, prove that with her it is not a case of sudden conversion. Did not the Church of Rome, one might even say, represent in the Middle Ages the rough plan of an international organization when kings and free communes equally submitted to a word from the Lateran?

Leo XIII, who, with Benedict XV, was the clearest mind that has ruled the Roman Church during the last two centuries, traced in 1894, in his letter *Praeclara gratulationis,* the following lines, to which the tragedy of 1914 imparts an almost prophetic savor: "For many long years we have been living in a peace more apparent than real. A prey to mutual suspicions, the Nations are smitten with the fever of armaments. . . . This state of armed peace has grown intolerable. But in order to put an end to ambitions, covetousness, rivalries, which are the kindlers of wars, we must come back to Christian virtues and, above all, to justice."

The same Pope, in reply to the Queen of Holland, who had invited him to lend his moral support to the Peace Conference of 1899, expressed himself as follows: "It is a noble idea and one closely connected with our ministry, which possesses a kind of high investiture as a Mediator of peace."

At the same time that the Pope was writing to Queen Wilhelmina, the Secretary of State, Cardinal Rampolla, was expressing to Count Mouravieff his hope that the Conference at the Hague "would succeed in settling the differences between the nations by the simple means of moral forces . . . the adoption of mediation and arbitration appearing to be the most suitable system."

The open political mind of Leo XIII, who was the first in modern times to use the expression "Societas Nationum" (Encyclical *In pluribus* of 1888) was entirely wanting in his successor Pius X; but the modest old Venetian curate had a sort of evangelic instinct that guided him to the same affirmations. When Andrew Carnegie founded the Endowment for

International Peace, Pius X wrote to the Apostolic Delegate for the United States: "We greatly congratulate ourselves on this initiative. No reasoning man can fail to approve of it, particularly We who represent Him who is the Prince and God of Peace."

Benedict XV succeeded Pius X at the moment when Belgium was invaded. The mind of this Pope, during the atrocious years of the War, was somewhat misunderstood by all of us. Our countries were struggling in the fiery furnace and we had, perhaps, the duty to be impassioned. He, who no longer belonged to any country, could, at the height of the War, in August, 1917, indite the message containing the famous phrase on "the useless slaughter," in which he proposed to the belligerents the threefold program: simultaneous and proportional decrease of armaments, compulsory arbitration, and international penalties.

Then came the peace. The Treaty of Versailles consecrated the newborn Society of Nations. A year passed by. Great states were hostile to it, or were excluded. Truly that would suffice to excuse or explain the coldness of the Holy See.

All the same, those who were already convinced of the supreme necessity for Europe to strive at Geneva, since Geneva existed, for an organization that would eliminate the dangers of new disasters, which might prove irreparable, were forced six years ago to the opinion that the Encyclical *Pacem Die* (May 23, 1920) unduly ignored the Genevan institution, in invoking (and by invoking, treating as not yet existing) the formation of a Society of Nations, to ensure their reciprocal independence. "The Church (to quote from the Encyclical) will certainly not refuse its contribution to *this* League between the Nations based on Christian law.'' Such a phrase proves enough the papal diffidence toward the League of Nations two years after the Treaty of Versailles.

A change has evidently taken place in the pontifical thought between the cold phrases of 1920 and the warm speeches of the Nuncios in 1927. Of course, it may be observed by Catholic dialecticians, principles remain always inviolate with the Church; it is only their empirical application that depends on times and opportunities.

Quite true. When the Church gives way, and when the change seems too sudden, she may always invoke age-old principles to justify it. This happened, to take an example in another field, a few months ago, when, contrary to all traditions and in spite of the mistrust of four centuries of Christianity in China, the Holy See raised to the rank of bishops a certain number of Chinese priests. It had never been done before because there had always been the not unreasonable fear that the unextirpated Buddhism and Confucianism which form the very essence of every Chinese being, might ultimately transform, unconsciously but fatally, the orthodoxy of the Catholic doctrine. But the Chinese revolution was there with its violent exclusiveness. Bishops were at once consecrated from among the Chinese, and to those who are surprised, evangelic texts are quoted amongst the flocks themselves. This does not, however, explain how it was that these texts remained unapplied until the advance of the Canton revolutionaries toward the Yangtze.

To return to our argument, the really important

point of the problem lies in the reasons that can have
led the Church to adopt her new attitude. It must be
admitted at once that it is reducing the preoccupations of the Papacy to the low level of the politicians
to see, in the recent manifestations, nothing more
than clever schemes for forming or strengthening,
on either side of the Rhine, political parties to serve
its own purposes. It is of some interest to note that
this has been hinted, with more or less of apparent
respect, especially by parties and papers who consider themselves as pillars of the Faith. It is frequently like that: under the cover of certain enthusi-
asms for the Church, or Monarchy, or any other old
institution, what in reality is hidden is the intention
of being served by them.

Let us seek higher and further for the reasons that
have decided the Roman Church to show Geneva an
active sympathy of which she was so chary six years
ago. During these six years, in fact, Geneva has
lived, which is a great deal for the Vatican; and
what is still more, with the entry of Germany it has
grown. But that is not all.

The Roman Church had already shown herself
aware, even before the oratorical manifestations in
Berlin and Paris, that the different nationalisms
which are making European life so difficult, might
end by becoming a danger to the education of those
new generations who, not having seen the War, have
the impression of a glorious adventure in which
there is everything to gain for one's country and
self. The solemn placing on the Index of the French
nationalist organ *L'Action française,* which preceded by a few days the speeches of the Nuncios, can

only, in reality, be explained by the Church's anxiety in this direction.[1]

It is the dread of a newly appearing type of pagan Catholicism that more than any other argument has decided the Church in favor of the Geneva atmosphere. It is the dread that this Catholicism, noisy as it is, trying as it does to catch adepts among the classes who so wrongly and so naïvely believe themselves to be conservative, may end by compromising the Church.

These dreads explain that the most important organ of the Catholic thought, the *Civiltà cattolica,* has gone so far as to express, in its number of last October, the deepest sympathy with the Congress for Peace which the *Internationale Democratique* held at Bierville, in France, last summer. In this article the *Civiltà cattolica* anticipates the doctrinal objections inspired by the traditional Catholic distrust toward any non-Catholic action. (This distrust is ordinarily inculcated into the faithful because it is considered that any contact with non-Catholics, even in the service of high moral ideas, like the League of Nations, contains the risk of weakening the sense of spiritual distance that members of the Church are ordered to feel toward outsiders.) The *Civiltà cattolica,* which is from its origins the organ of the Jesuits, in this case reassures our minds, by this *Distinguo* in which I leave it to you to look or not for the smell of the Jesuitical traditions illustrated by Pascal in his immortal *Provinciales:*

"Unless we deceive ourselves, there is a great difference between error and errants (*tra errore e*

[1] See also Document IX, p. 124.

erranti). With error there can be, it is clear, no contact, no alliance, for light and darkness are ever mu-
tually repellant. To the errants, on the other hand,
we can always throw out bridges, and, on occasions,
must do so, if it is true that the individual man is not
the personification of error and evil.''

The same article finishes with these phrases which
afford clear proof of the distrust entertained by
the Vatican for the excesses of nationalistic doctrines: ''We would fain hope that the number of men
of good will who are rich in a realistic not less than
in an optimistic sense, increases more and more, and
that the particularist and immoderately national
spirit that still dominates too many consciences, is at
last opening to a true view of international life. To
contribute to this education is the grandest mission
of the present time. The Rome of the Caesars could
only discover 'Si vis pacem para bellum.' The Rome
of the Popes offers us the more human and Christian
teaching: 'Si vis pacem, para pacem.' ''

If in France they had known and pondered more
the expressions used in a paper so authorized, it is
probable that less surprise would have been felt at
the Paris speech of last January.

The essential words had already been uttered. The
same *Civiltà cattolica* had, in a previous number,
gone so far as to say: ''Bolsheviks who dream of
imposing their Utopias upon the world, nationalists
who, in a spirit of paganism, deify the national
reality, have wished to sing a requiem on Wilson's
work. We can in no way join their chorus, behind
which are vibrating the passions that prepare and
hasten bloody catastrophes. If an attempt is made
to weaken or overthrow the League of Nations, the

Catholics must rally to its defense. It must not die, but improve and live.''

What is meant by the word ''improve?'' Are those right who think that, after the Papal manifestation of January 1, the Holy See intends, while at the same time striving for other contingent results, to enter the League of Nations?

The Church of Rome is in reality much more a state than many states consisting of territories and citizens. She therefore pursues a policy which is dictated to her, according to the time, by the conceptions she forms of her interests as a state. But, in certain questions of principle she never changes. When the Pope, in his letter to the Queen of Holland, declared himself to be the holder of a ''high investiture as mediator of peace,'' he did not make use of a vague literary phrase. It was a prudent echo, such as the times permit, of the traditions of the great epoch of the Gregory's and Innocent's, traditions that still retained sufficient power even in the century of the miscreant Machiavelli, for Alexander VI to be able to draw lines for the division of American lands across the Atlantic. It is difficult to believe that, even if invited, the Holy See could enter Geneva as *inter pares*.

If the offer were made to him it is very unlikely that the Pope would explain to poor profane ears the reasons that would be dictated to him by a long theocratic exclusivism. He would not be wanting in logical reasons for his refusal, beginning with Article 16 of the Covenant, which imposes the contribution of material concerted action against any State that might break its international pledges by an attempt against the peace. The Papacy has indeed summoned armies to fight against other armies, the last instance being the French intervention against our Mazzini's Roman troops in 1848, when it was a question of destroying the newborn republic and reëstablishing papal rule. But under the new conditions in which it finds itself, it would have everything to lose by being obliged to participate, were it even by moral assent, in measures of repression and coercion.

Even its occasional collaboration in the labors undertaken by the League, collaboration that has recently been frequently accorded, will not fail to be accompanied by sentiments of prudent reserve. It is natural that the Holy See should desire, for reasons of prestige, that such a great human Areopagus should publicly solicit its official collaboration. But, to quote an example which only to the profane may seem secondary, the Church of Rome will regard with distrust certain projects of the League of Nations, such as the reform of the calendar. If she collaborates therein, it will be merely for the purpose of watching. The recollection of the *decadis* of the French Terror is today for us a picturesque episode. It remains for the Church, a shameful souvenir connected with the worshiping of the Goddess of Reason, as burning and fresh as if of yesterday.

But let us drop secondary questions. It is time to come to a conclusion. What is certain is—I think I have demonstrated it—that the oldest of all religious and, if you like, political institutions, in the western world has at last taken sides, in spite of her traditional prudence, in the great quarrel: the only one quarrel that matters for our future civilization. She has understood that the nervous starts of certain heated nationalisms—artificial as they are—

may bring the peace into danger. She has realized
that there will be either peace, with its uncertainties,
its ups and downs, its painful social struggles, but
for all that, peace, with an assured future of a life of
progress and human dignity, or else another war,
and, with the war, the merited destruction of a civilization that has degenerated into a brutal, material
impetus without any common moral rule of life.
When that happens it will be useless to look for reactionary police measures against the obscure forces
of a new system of oriental slavery which—to the
parties and men afraid of liberty—seemed, a few
years ago, to be there, knocking at our doors from
the East. There are no Chinese walls, no barbed
wires, no *ententes* between so-called strong governments that may be able to keep back the human tide
toward a new form of hope, if the enraged nationalisms and imperialisms are going to provoke a new
bankruptcy of the European civilization. These, and
these alone, are the accomplices and the allies of the
so-called Russian danger.

All our precautions would be like sand banks
against the sea. There is only one way: to realize at
last, and not only in the official phrases, that the true
prosperity of our nations is dependent upon the
prosperity of the neighbors; that we will find all together our salvation, or we will sink together. This
we have refused to learn out of love. Maybe we are
going to learn it, out of stern necessity, out of fear.

May it be!

DOCUMENTS

I

TEXT OF COUNT SFORZA'S PROPOSAL FOR THE SOLUTION OF THE UPPER SILESIAN QUESTION

(Translated from Italian)

THE fact that so large a part of French public opinion is highly aroused, makes action by Italy, who above all desires peace, all the wiser. Even the question of dividing the mining region becomes less important in comparison to the dangers which threaten the general situation.

Regarding as fundamental the principles of respect for treaties and of nationality, I propose the following:

The persistent aggravation of the situation in Upper Silesia makes a prompt solution of the question advisable. But a meeting of the Supreme Council at this moment is impossible—particularly as it might only serve to increase further the tension between London and Paris. It is therefore timely to settle the question through direct agreement between the three Allied Governments, the British, French, and Italian, on the following basis and on the premises recognized by the three governments:

1. that the question of Upper Silesia ought to be determined according to the principles set up by the Treaty and according to the results of the plebiscite.

2. that neither Poland nor Germany ought to take the law into their own hands.

Inasmuch as the plebiscite has given to Germany less than 60 per cent of the individual votes, with majorities in less than 55 per cent of the communes, it would seem just to mark the frontier in such a way as to give to Germany and to Poland territories as far as possible proportional to the results of the plebiscite both in respect to area and to population.

As bases for discussion rather than as definite proposals, I offer these two formulas:

1a

Poland shall have the southern part of the Circle of Ratibor, on the right bank of the Oder, the Circle of Rybnik minus the northwestern salient traversed by the Ratibor-Gleiwitz railroad, which shall remain German; the Circles of Kattowitz, Königshütte, Beuthen and Tarnowitz, the extreme southwestern rural section of the Circle of Gleiwitz and the southern point of the Zabrze district; the eastern part of the Lublinitz district including Stahlhammer. This solution will divide the industrial region leaving Gleiwitz and Zabrze to Germany.

1b

Poland shall receive territory according to the preceding formula minus Königshütte, the parts of the Circles of Beuthen and Kattowitz lying between Königshütte and the Circle of Zabrze. In compensation she shall receive the eastern part of the Circles of Lublinitz and Rosenberg, with the two principal towns, in such a way as to hold all the railroad which connects Beuthen with Poland.

This solution will leave a much larger part of the industrial region to Germany and will require a more complicated frontier, but it will assign to Poland an important railroad.

The exchange of views between the three governments, British, French and Italian, as well as the eventual deliberation to be left to the Council of Ambassadors, should be carried on with the utmost secrecy in order to guard against dangerous reactions in Upper Silesia.

As soon as a definite decision has been reached it should be communicated to the governments at Berlin and Warsaw, who will proceed to occupy their respective zones with regular troops.

II

ANTI-HAPSBURG CONVENTION

NOVEMBER 12, 1920

(The official text is in Italian)[1]

In order to ensure the blessings of peace the Italian Government and the Government of the State of the Serbs, Croats, and Slovenes have decided to stipulate the following convention, and have appointed, for the Italian Government, Mr. Giovanni Giolitti, Deputy to Parliament, Prime Minister, Count Carlo Sforza, Senator, Minister for Foreign Affairs, Doctor Ivanoe Bonomi, Minister of War; for the Serb-Croat-Slovene State, Mr. Vesnitch, Prime Minister, Doctor Ante Trumbitch, Minister for Foreign Affairs, Mr. Stoyanovitch, Minister of Commerce, who have agreed on the following principles:

I. The two Governments pledge themselves jointly to take all political measures calculated to prevent the restoration of the House of Hapsburg either to the throne of Austria or that of Hungary;

II. The two Governments pledge themselves to afford, each to the other, such diplomatic assistance as is most suitable to attain the above aim;

III. The two Governments pledge themselves to mark all activities directed against their reciprocal safety, whether coming from Austrian or from Hungarian territory, and to that end they will maintain the closest possible contact with each other.

IV. The Italian Government, which has learned with satisfaction the understanding established between the

---

[1] The Yugoslav plenipotentiaries accepted the Italian text as the binding text and did not insist on a parallel Serbian text, as, according to diplomatic tradition, they were entitled to do. The same happened for the treaty of peace between Italy and Yugoslavia signed at Rapallo on the same day.

Serb-Croat-Slovene Government and the Czechoslovak Government (exclusively with the same object as the present Agreement), and the Serb-Croat-Slovene Government, will bring this convention to the knowledge of the Czechoslovak Government.

V. This agreement will remain in force during two years after the exchange of the ratifications, and will be renewed, if not denounced six months before.

VI. The present agreement shall be ratified as soon as possible and the ratifications will take place in Rome. Rapallo, 12 November 1920.

(signed)   G. GIOLITTI   VESNITCH
C. SFORZA   A. TRUMBITCH
I. BONOMI   STOYANOVITCH

III

ITALO-CZECHOSLOVAK AGREEMENT

FEBRUARY 8, 1921

Exchange of letters of the two Foreign Ministers

I

Rome, 8 février 1921.

Monsieur le Ministre, Je suis heureux d'être dans le cas d'avoir pu constater, pendant les conversations que j'ai eu avec Votre Excellence, la parfaite identité des vues et des lignes directrices dans le domaine de la politique extérieure de nos deux Pays,—identité qui est une consequence des intérets communs de nos deux peuples et apparait encore plus évidente quand il s'agit de l'application des traités de paix et de la politique à suivre envers les Etats successeurs de la monarchie austro-hongroise, parceque les buts auxquels nous tendons dans l'intéret de la sécurité et la prosperité de nos peuples sont en parfaite concordance.

Je me rejouis de cette constatation, d'autant plus qu'elle est une garantie de l'accord et de la collaboration politique des deux Etats encore plus efficace que celle qui pourrait resulter des dispositions spéciales d'une Convention.

Mais considérant le fait que les frontières italiennes ont été fixées par la conclusion du traité de Rapallo entre l'Italie et l'Etat des Serbes, Croates et Slovenes et qu'à cette occasion une Convention speciale de caractère politique a été conclue, il est natural que la communication faite au Gouvernement Tchecoslovaque sur le fondement de l'article 4 de la même Convention acquière la signification que les accords et les engagements y contenus sont valables également pour l'Italie et la Tchecoslovaque.

Agréez, Monsieur le Ministre, les assurances de ma très-haute considération.

SFORZA.

II

Rome, 8 février 1921.

Monsieur le Ministre, J'ai l'honneur de Vous accuser reception de Votre note, dont texte suit:

(Here follows reproduction of preceding letter)

Je suis heureux de pouvoir communiquer à Votre Excellence que mon Gouvernement est en plein accord avec le contenu de la note ci-dessus et je prie Votre Excellence de vouloir bien agréer l'expression de ma très-haute considération.

EDOUARD BENES.

IV

ITALO-TURKISH AGREEMENT FOR ITALIAN ECONOMIC DEVELOPMENT IN ANATOLIA

MARCH 13, 1921

(To take the place, as a free agreement, of the Tripartite Agreement between Great Britain, France, and Italy, made without Turkey's previous knowledge.)

Son Excellence le Comte Sforza, Président de la Delegation Italienne et Ministre des Affairs Etrangères du Royaume d'Italie d'une part, et Son Excellence Bekir Sami Bey, Président de la Delegation de la grande assemblee nationale et Ministre des Affaires Etrangères de Turquie d'autre part, sont convenus des dispositions suivantes:

1. Collaboration économique Italo-Turque avec droit de priorité pour les concessions d'ordre économique à accorder par l'Etat en vue de la mise en valeur et du developpement économique dans les Sandjaks d'Adalia, Bourdour, Houghla, Isparta et d'une part des Sandjaks d'Afion-Kara-Hissar et de Kutahya, Aidin et Konia à déterminer dans l'accord définitif, dans la mesure ou cela ne serait pas effective directement par le gouvernement Ottoman ou les réssortissants Ottomans à l'aide de capitaux nationaux. Concession à un groupe Italo-Turc de la mine houilliere d'Heraclée dont la limite sera déterminée dans la carte qui sera jointe a l'accord définitif.

2. Les concessions comportant monopole ou privilège, seront exploitées par des sociétés constituées selon la loi ottomane.

3. Association la plus large possible de capitaux ottomans et italiens (la participation pouvant aller jusqu'à 50%).

4. Le gouvernement royal d'Italie s'engage à appuyer éfficacement auprès de ses alliés toutes les demandes de la Delegation Turque rélativement au traité de paix, spécialement la restitution à la Turquie de la Thrace et de Smyrne.

5. Le gouvernement royal d'Italie donne une assurance formelle que, au plus tard à la ratification de la paix, et d'après un accord entré les deux pays, il procédera au rappel de ses troupes actuellement sur le térritoire ottoman.

6. Les dispositions ci-haut formulées seront mises en vigueur en vertu d'une convention, qui sera stipulée entre les deux parties contractantes, immediatement après la conclusion d'une paix assurant à la Turquie une existence viable et independante et acceptée par elle.

Fait à Londres, en double exemplaire le 13 Mars, 1921.

Signé: SFORZA
S. BEKIR

V

TREATY OF DEFENSIVE ALLIANCE BETWEEN LATVIA AND ESTHONIA

NOVEMBER 1, 1923

Fermement résolues de sauvegarder leur souveraineté nationale et l'indépendance acquises au prix de tant de sacrifices ainsi que l'intégrité de leurs territoires la République d'Esthonie et la République de Lettonie ont décidé de conclure un traité d'alliance défensive.

Dans ce but ont été nommé en qualité de délégués plénipotentiaires, savoir
de la part de l'Esthonie
Monsieur Fr. AKEL, Ministre des Affaires Etrangères,
de la part de la Lettonie
Monsieur Z. A. MEIEROVICS, Président du Conseil, Ministre des Affaires Etrangères.
lesquels, après s'être communiqué leurs pleins pouvoirs, trouvés en bonne et due forme, sont convenus des dispositions suivantes:

Article 1

Les Hautes Parties Contractantes s'engagent à suivre une politique purement pacifique ayant pour but de maintenir et de resserrer les liens d'amitié ainsi que de développer les relations économiques avec toutes les nations et surtout entre les Etats Baltiques et les pays voisins.

Article 2

Afin de coordonner leurs efforts pacifiques, les deux Gouvernements s'engagent à se concerter sur les questions de politique extérieure d'une importance commune et à se prêter une aide réciproque politique et diplomatique dans leurs rapports internationaux.

Article 3

Les Hautes Parties Contractantes s'engagent à s'aider réciproquement dans le cas où l'une d'elles serait attaquée, sans provocation de sa part sur ses frontières actuelles.

En conséquence, au cas où l'une des Hautes Parties Contractantes serait attaquée sans provocation de sa part, l'autre se considérera en état de guerre et lui prêtera une assistance armée.

Article 4

Les autorités techniques compétentes de la République esthonienne et de la République lettone fixeront d'un commun accord la manière dont les deux pays se prêteront assistance et les dispositions nécessaires pour l'exécution de l'article 3 du présent traité.

Article 5

Si les Hautes Parties Contractantes, malgré leurs efforts pacifiques, se trouvaient en état de guerre défensive conformément à l'article 3, ils s'engagent à ne traiter ni conclure l'armistice ni la paix l'une sans l'autre.

Article 6

Toutes les questions litigieuses qui pourraient surgir entre les Hautes Parties Contractantes et qui ne peuvent pas être résolues par voies diplomatiques, seront portées devant la Cour de Justice Internationale ou soumises à un arbitrage international.

Article 7

Aucune des Hautes Parties Contractantes ne pourra conclure une alliance avec une tierce puissance sans le consentement de l'autre. Elles s'engagent à communiquer dès à présent l'une à l'autre le texte des traités conclus entre l'une d'elles et un ou plusieurs autres Etats.

Article 8

La durée du présent traité est de dix ans à partir du jour de l'échange des instruments de ratification. Ce terme expiré chacune des deux Parties Contractantes aura la faculté de la dénoncer en avisant l'autre Partie un an d'avance.

Article 9

Le présent traité sera communiqué à la Société des Nations dans le but d'y être enregistré et publié.

Article 10

Le présent traité sera ratifié et les instruments de ratification seront échangés dans le plus bref délai à Riga.

En foi de quoi les plénipotentiaires ont signé le présent traité et y ont apposé leurs sceaux. Fait en double exemplaire à Tallinn le Ier novembre mil neuf cent vingt trois.

FR. AKEL   Z. A. MEIEROVICS.

VI

CONVENTION OF CONCILIATION AND ARBITRATION BETWEEN ESTHONIA, FINLAND, LATVIA, AND POLAND

January 17, 1925

Les Républiques d'Esthonie, de Finlande, de Lettonie et de Pologne, décidés à développer les relations amicales qui existent entre Elles et décidées à donner, dans leurs rapports réciproques, la plus large application au principe du règlement des différends internationaux par des moyens pacifiques, ont résolu de conclure une Convention de conciliation et d'arbitrage. A cet effet ont été nommés Plénipotentiaries :

par le Président de la République d'Esthonie :

Monsieur C. R. Pusta, Ministre des Affaires Etrangères.

par le Président de la République de Finlande :

Monsieur Hj. J. Procopé, Ministre des Affaires Etrangères.

par le Président de la République de Lettonie :

Monsieur S. Meierovics, Ministre des Affaires Etrangères.

par le Président de la République de Pologne :

Monsieur le Comte A. Skrzynski, Ministre des Affaires Etrangères,

lesquels Plénipotentiaires, dûment autorisés, sont convenus des articles suivants :

Article 1

Les Hautes Parties Contractantes désirant appliquer dans leurs rapports mutuels les principes dominants du Pacte de la Société des Nations développés par le Protocole de Genève adopté le 2 octobre 1924, sont résolues à se servir des moyens y prévus pour le règlement pacifique des conflits qui pourraient surgir entre Elles.

Article 2

Les Hautes Parties Contractantes s'engagent à soumettre à une procédure de conciliation ou à l'arbitrage tous les différends qui pourraient s'élever entre Elles et n'auraient pu être réglés par la voie diplomatique dans un délai raisonnable. Toutefois l'engagement précité ne se rapportera ni aux questions qui de par leur nature juridique relèvent uniquement de la législation interne de la Partie en cause ni aux différends concernant le Statut territorial des Hautes Parties Contractantes.

Tout différend susceptible d'être régléde la manière indiquée ci-dessus sera soumis à une procédure de conciliation, à moins que les Parties en litige ne conviennent de le soumettre immédiatement à l'arbitrage.

Au cas où le rapport élaboré par la Commission de conciliation instituée en vertu de l'article 6 de la présente Convention n'aurait pas été accepté par toutes les Parties en litige, le différend sera soumis à l'arbitrage, si l'une des Parties le demande.

Article 3

S'il s'agit d'un différend qui, à teneur de la législation interne de l'une des Hautes Parties Contractantes, relève de la compétence des tribunaux, les tribunaux administratifs y compris, la Partie défenderesse pourra s'opposer à ce qu'il soit soumis à l'arbitrage ou à une procédure de conciliation avant qu'un jugement définitif ait été rendu par l'autorité judiciare compétente.

Article 4

Dans le cas où le recours à une procédure arbitrale serait prévu dans une convention antérieurement conclue dont ne font partie que les Etats signataires de la présente Convention, il est convenu que tout différend auquel la convention antérieure s'appliquerait, sera soumis par les Etats entre lesquels le conflit est surgi à une commission de conciliation ou à l'arbitrage, conformément à la présente Convention.

Article 5

Il est entendu que les obligations assumées par les Hautes
Parties Contractantes en vertu de la présente Convention
n'entravent aucunement leur faculté de soumettre, d'un
commun accord, un différend qui aurait pu surgir entre
Elles, à la Cour permanente de Justice Internationale.

Article 6

Les Hautes Parties Contractantes établiront dans les trois
mois du dépôt de la dernière ratification de la présente Convention une Commission permanente de conciliation, com-
posée de quatre membres, à raison d'un membre nommé par
chacune d'Elles, et d'un président désigné d'un commun
accord parmi les ressortissants d'un Etat tiers. A défaut
d'entente entre les Parties, le Président sera nommé, à la
requête de l'une d'Elles, par le Président de la Cour permanente de Justice Internationale.

La partie désirant soumettre un différend à la procédure
de conciliation s'adressera au Président de la Commission
permanente. Celui-ci portera immédiatement cette notifica-
tion à la connaissance de la Partie ou des Parties adverses
et invitera les Parties en litige à compléter le nombre des
membres nommés par Elles par des membres supplémentaires ad hoc, à raison d'un membre pour chaque Partie en
litige, ces derniers membres devant être choisis parmi les
ressortissants d'un Etat tiers et nommés dans un sants d'un
Etat tiers et nommés dans un délai ne dépassant pas six
semaines, à compter du jour de l'invitation. Au cas où la
nomination n'aurait pas eu lieu dans le délai prescrit, les
membres supplémentaires seront désignés par le Président.

Les membres permanents de la Commission nommés par
les Parties en litige ainsi que les membres supplémentaires
seront convoqués sans retard par le Président et constitue-
ront ensemble avec lui la Commission nommés par les Parties en litige ainsi différend soumis à la procédure de conciliation.

Article 7

Toute commission de conciliation connait de sa compétence d'après les articles précédents.

Si l'un des Etats entre lesquels un conflit est surgi l'avait soumis à une procédure de conciliation et si la Partie adverse faisant valoir la compétence de la Cour permanente de Justice Internationale, cette compétence étant, dans le cas donné, obligatoire pour les Parties, lui soumettait le même différend, l'examen de celui-ci sera suspendu jusqu'à ce que la Cour ait statué sur sa compétence.

La requête ainsi adressée à la Cour par l'une des Parties suspendra les mesures prévues à l'article 6, jusqu'à ce que la Cour ait statué sur sa compétence.

Article 8

Les membres de la Commission permanente seront nommés pour trois ans. Sauf accord contraire entre les Hautes Parties Contractantes, ils ne pourront pas être révoqués pendant la durée de leur mandat. En cas de décès ou de retraite de l'un d'eux il devra être pourvu à son remplacement pour le reste de la durée de son mandat, si possible dans les deux mois qui suivront et, en tout cas, aussitôt qu'un différend aura été soumis à la Commission.

Article 9

Si, à l'expiration du mandat d'un membre de la commission permanente, il n'est pas pourvu à son remplacement, son mandat est censé renouvelé pour une période de trois ans: toutefois, sur la demande de l'une des Parties les fonctions du Président doivent cesser à la fin de son mandat.

Un membre dont le mandat expire pendant la durée d'une procédure en cours continue à prendre part à l'examen du différend jusqu'à ce que la procédure soit terminée, nonobstant le fait que son remplaçant ait été désigné.

Article 10

Dans un délai de quinze jours, à dater de celui où l'un des

Etats Contractants aura porté un différend devant la Commission, chacune des Parties pourra pour l'examen du litige visé, remplacer le membre permanent désigné par Elle par une personne possédant une compétence spéciale dans la matière.

La Partie qui voudrait user de ce droit, en avertira immédiatement la Partie adverse; dans ce cas, celle-ci a la faculté d'user du droit dans un délai de quinze jours à partir de celui où l'avertissement Lui est parvenu.

Article 11

La Commission se réunit dans l'endroit que les Parties désignent d'un commun accord ou, à défaut d'accord, au siège de la Société des Nations.

La Commission pourra, si elle le juge nécessaire, se réunir dans un autre endroit.

Article 12

Les Parties en litige fourniront à la Commission toutes les informations utiles et lui faciliteront, à tous égards, l'accomplissement de sa tâche.

La Commission pourra, le cas échéant, demander au Secrétaire Général de la Société des Nations l'assistance du Secrétariat, si la Commission en a besoin pour ses travaux.

Article 13

La procédure devant la Commission est contradictoire.

A défaut d'une décision contraire prise à l'unanimité, les dispositions contenues aux titres III et IV de la Convention de la Haye pour le règlement pacifique des conflits internationaux, du 18 octobre 1907, seront appliquées à la procédure devant la Commission.

Les débats ne sont publics que si la Commission, d'accord avec les Parties, en décide ainsi.

Article 14

Les décisions de la Commission sont prises à la majorité. Chaque membre dispose d'une voix, celle du Président étant décisive en cas de partage. La Commission ne peut prendre des décisions portant sur le fond du différend que si tous les membres sont présents.

Article 15

La Commission fera un rapport sur le différend qui lui a été soumis. Le rapport comportera un projet de règlement du différend, si les circonstances y donnent lieu et si trois au moins des membres de la Commission, le Président étant considéré comme membre, se mettent d'accord sur un tel projet.

L'avis motivé des membres restés en minorité sera consigné dans le rapport.

Article 16

Sous réserve du droit des Parties en litige de prolonger ce délai, la Commission doit achever ses travaux dans un délai de six mois, à compter du jour de la première réunion de la Commission.

Le temps durant lequel les travaux de la Commission sont suspendus selon les dispositions de l'article 7 n'est pas compris dans le délai susmentionné.

Article 17

Le rapport de la Commission est signé par le Président et porté sans délai à la connaissance des Parties en litige et du Secrétaire général de la Société des Nations.

Article 18

Les Parties, dont le différend a été soumis à la Commission, porteront à Leur connaissance réciproque, ainsi qu'à la connaissance du Président de la Commission permanente, dans un délai raisonnable, si Elles acceptent les constatations du rapport et les propositions qu'il renferme.

Il appartient aux Parties en litige de décider, d'un commun accord, si le rapport de la Commission doit être publié immédiatement. A défaut d'un accord, la Commission pourra, en cas de raisons spéciales, procéder à la publication du rapport.

Article 19

Lorsque, en vertu des dispositions de l'article 2, un différend sera soumis à l'arbitrage, le Tribunal arbitral sera établi par l'accord des Parties.

A défaut de constitution du Tribunal par l'accord des Parties, il sera procédé de la manière suivante :

Chaque Partie nommera deux arbitres dont l'un doit être pris sur la liste des membres de la Cour permanente d'arbitrage et choisi à l'exclusion de ses propres nationaux. Les arbitres ainsi désignés choisiront ensemble le Président du Tribunal. En cas de partage des voix, le choix du Président est confié au Président de la Cour Permanente de Justice Internationale.

Article 20

Lorsqu'il y aura lieu à un arbitrage entre les Parties en litige, Elles établiront, dans un délai de trois mois au plus tard, un compromis spécial concernant l'objet du litige ainsi que les modalités de la procédure. A défaut de clauses compromissoires contraires, Elles se conformeront pour tout ce qui concerne la procédure arbitrale aux dispositions établies par la convention signée à la Haye le 18 octobre 1907 pour le réglement pacifique des conflits internationaux y compris les articles 53 et 54 et tenant compte de l'article 83 de ladite convention.

Article 21

La sentence arbitrale est obligatoire. Si, toutefois, la sentence établissait qu'une décision d'une instance judiciare ou de toute autre autorité relevant de l'une des Hautes Parties Contractantes se trouve entièrement ou partiellement en opposition avec le droit international, et si le droit constitutionnel de cette Partie ne permettait pas ou ne permettait qu'imparfaitement d'effacer par voie administrative les conséquences de la décision dont il s'agit, il sera accordé à la Partie lésée une satisfaction équitable d'un autre ordre.

Article 22

Les Parties s'abstiendront, durant le cours de la procédure de conciliation ou d'arbitrage, de toute mesure pouvant avoir une répercussion préjudiciable sur l'acceptation des propositions de la Commission ou sur l'exécution de la sentence.

Article 23

Chacune des Parties indemnisera les membres de la Commission ainsi que les arbitres nommés par Elle ou désignés, faute de nomination, par le Président, conformément à l'article 6. L'indemnité du Président sera fournie par les Parties en litige en proportion égale.

Les Parties doivent chercher à s'entendre pour que les indemnités soient fixées d'après les mêmes principes.

Chaque Partie supportera les frais de procédure encourus par Elle, ceux déclarés communs par la Commission ou le tribunal seront supportés par les Parties en proportion égale.

Article 24

Les dispositions de la présente Convention seront applicables même si les différends qui viendraient à s'élever avaient leur origine dans des faits antérieurs à sa conclusion.

Article 25

Il est entendu que la présente Convention n'apportera aucune modification aux obligations des Etats signataires fondées sur le Protocole pour le règlement pacifique des différends internationaux, adopté à Genève le 2 octobre 1924.

Article 26

Tout différend relatif à l'interprétation de la présente Convention sera soumis à la Cour permanente de Justice Internationale.

Article 27

La présente Convention sera ratifiée et les ratifications seront déposées à Helsinki (Helsingfors) aussitôt que faire se pourra. Elle entrera en vigueur immédiatement après le dépôt des ratifications et aura une durée de trois années à dater du dépôt des ratifications accompli par tous les Etats signataires. Si elle n'a pas été dénoncée six mois au moins avant l'expiration de ce délai, elle restera en vigueur pendant une nouvelle période de trois ans et sera ainsi de suite censée renouvelée chaque fois pour trois ans, sauf dénonciation six mois au moins avant l'expiration de la précédente période de trois ans.

Nonobstant la dénonciation par l'une des Hautes Parties Contractantes, la Convention demeurera en vigueur en ce qui concerne les Parties qui ne l'auront pas dénoncée.

En foi de quoi les Plénipotentiaires respectifs ont signé la présente Convention et y ont apposé leurs cachets.

Fait à Helsinki (Helsingfors) en quatre originaux, le 17 janvier, de l'an 1925.

C. R. PUSTA.
HJ. J. PROCOPÉ.
Z. A. MEIEROVICS.
AL. SKRZYNSKI.

VII

PROJECT OF BALTIC PROTOCOL STUDIED BY THE BALTIC DELEGATES AT GENEVA IN 1925, WITH THE COLLABORATION OF THE POLISH MINISTER OF FOREIGN AFFAIRS

Considérant

les progrès réalisés par chacun des Pays Participants dans l'organsation de sa vie nationale, comme d'autre part la consolidation de la situation politique générale dans l'Europe orientale.

Estimant

que cet état de choses résulte en partie de la politique de collaboration suivie par ces Etats au cours des cinq derniéres années.

.   .   .   .   .

Les Ministres des Affaires Etrangères d'Esthonie, de Finlande, de Lettonie et de Pologne déclarent enregistrer avec la plus vive satisfaction les résultats heureux de la collaboration des quatre Etats Participants au cours des appréciant à leur juste valeur les fruits de cette collaboration passée et le grand intérêt que présente pour chacun des Pays Participants sa continuation à l'avenir,

conviennent de fixer les lignes générales de leur collaboration future et de signer l'accord ci-après qu'ils s'engagent à soumettre à l'agrément de leurs Parlements respectifs.

(a) Les H.P.C. s'engagent à poursuivre entre eux la collaboration loyale et confiante inaugurée par la conférence d'Helsingfors du 15 Janvier 1920 et continuée dans les conférences consécutives. Elles affirmerent à nouveau leur volonté de compléter autant que possible afin de fixer sur de solides bases juridiques leurs relations mutuelles, le système de traités, accords et conventions les liant entre elles, ainsi que de tendre leurs efforts vers une action commune dans le domaine de la politique internationale. Elles considèrent comme un devoir stricte de se communiquer dés leur ratification tous les traités, accords et conventions que chacune d'Elles contractera avec toute Puissance étrangère.

(b) Dans l'application de la Convention d'Arbitrage et de Conciliation, signée à Helsingfors le 17 Janvier 1925, elles s'inspireront des mêmes sentiments qui ont présidé à son élaboration, et verront dans les organismes y prévus de véritables institutions de paix chargées de la mission de maintenir entre Elles l'entente et l'harmonie.

(c) Parfaitement conscientes des obligations que leur crée leur qualité de membres de la S. d. N., les H.P.C. confirment leur volonté de remplir dans leur plénitude ces obligations dans leurs relations mutuelles afin de pouvoir béné-

ficier dans une mesure équivalente des avantages corre-
spondants, spécialement en ce qui concerne la garantie de
leur sécurité et de leur indépendance ainsi que le maintien
de la paix dans l'Europe orientale.

(d) La collaboration entre les H.P.C. se poursuivra in-
dépendamment de la forme normale des relations diplomatiques, dans des conférences périodiques des quatre Etats.
Ces Conférences se tiendrent, suivant le principe déjà
établi, deux fois par an.

(e) Le présent accord est ouvert à l'adhésion de tout
Etat limitrophe de l'une des H.P.C. qui s'inspirerait des
mêmes principes d'entente et de collaboration, sous réserve
du consentement des Etats Signataires.

VIII

TREATY FOR THE EXECUTION OF THE CUSTOMS
UNION BETWEEN ESTHONIA AND LATVIA

FEBRUARY 5, 1927

Le Gouvernement de la République d'Esthonie et le
Gouvernement de la République de Lettonie animés du
désir d'étendre leur collaboration économique au delà des
limites fixées dans le traité préliminaire d'Union économique et douanière entre l'Esthonie et la Lettonie, signé à
Tallinn le Ier novembre 1923, ont résolu de conclure à cet
effet un Traité ayant pour but l'Union douanière entre les
deux Etats et ont désigné à cet effet pour leurs Plénipotentiaires, savoir:

Le Gouvernement de la République d'Esthonie
   M. AKEL, Ministre des Affaires Etrangères
Le Gouvernement de la République de Lettonie
   M. CIELENS, Ministre des Affaires Etrangères
lesquels, après s'être communiqué leurs pleins pouvoirs
trouvés en bonne et due forme, se sont mis d'accord sur les
dispositions suivantes:

Article 1

Dès l'entrée en vigueur du présent Traité, le Traité préliminaire d'union économique et douanière entre l'Esthonie et la Lettonie, signé à Tallinn le Ier novembre 1923, est considéré comme abrogé.

Un mois après l'entrée en vigueur des lois, conventions et arrangements prévus par l'article 6 pp. 1-7, sauf les exceptions prévues par l'art. 8, alinéa 4, une union douanière est établie entre la République d'Esthonie et la République de Lettonie et les territoires des deux Etats Contractants seront considérés comme ne formant qu'un seul territoire au point de vue de la douane. La perception des droits de douane sur les marchandises allant du territoire de l'un des pays au territoire de l'autre sera supprimée.

Article 2

Chacune des Parties Contractantes s'engage à accorder sur son territoire aux ressortissants de l'autre le même traitement qu'à ses nationaux en tout ce qui concerne l'utilisation, la possession et la disposition des biens immeubles, le commerce, l'industrie, la navigation, la juridiction et l'application des règlements administratifs ainsi que tous les impôts quel que soit leur caractère. Toutefois en ce qui concerne l'acquisition des biens immeubles, la fondation des sociétés anonymes et autres sociétés et associations commerciales, industrielles, financières ou d'assurance, la pêche, la construction navale nationale, le cabotage et le remorquage, les Parties Contractantes ne se garantissent réciproquement que le traitement qui est réservé aux ressortissants et aux personnes juridiques de la Nation la plus favorisée.

Article 3

Les ressortissants de chacune des Parties Contractantes seront réciproquement exempts de tout service militaire personnel, de la participation aux organisations militaires ainsi que de toute contribution militaire, soit en argent, soit en nature.

Dans un but militaire, ils ne pourront être soumis à des obligations de service et de réquisition autres que celles qui incombent aux citoyens du Pays et ils ont, sur base de réciprocité, droit à la rétribution prévue pour les nationaux de chacun des deux Pays.

Ils seront également dispensés de toute charge et de toute fonction judiciaire ou municipale quelconque.

Article 4

Les certificats de jauge délivrés par les autorités compétentes de l'une des Parties Contractantes seront acceptés par l'autre Partie, si le jaugeage a été exécuté d'après le système Moorsom.

Article 5

Les Parties Contractantes procèderont sans délai à la nomination d'une Commission générale mixte et paritaire, chargée, conformément aux dispositions du présent Traité, de l'exécution des travaux préliminaires de l'union douanière esto-lettonne. La Commission générale se mettra d'accord sur le règlement d'ordre intérieur. Pour faciliter ses travaux, la Commission générale est autorisée à procéder à la nomination de sous-commissions spéciales.

Article 6

La Commission générale sera chargée :

(1) d'élaborer un tarif douanier commun estho-letton ;
(2) d'unifier la législation douanière des deux Etats ;
(3) d'unifier la législation concernant les accises et les monopoles des deux Etats ;
(4) d'unifier les tarifs de transport et de communication des deux Etats, notamment ceux de chemins de fer, de navigation, d'aéronautique, des postes, télégraphes, téléphones et T.S.F. ;
(5) de régler la question des recettes douanières de façon qu'une compensation réciproque juste soit atteinte après constatation soit par l'enregistrement des marchandises allant du territoire de l'un des pays au

territoire de l'autre, soit par d'autres méthodes ap-
propriées, des pertes fiscales éventuelles des deux
Etats;

(6) d'unifier la législation concernant les impôts, les
contributions directes et les brevets de commerce,
ainsi que la législation concernant la protection du
travail;

(7) de coordonner la politique d'émission et d'escompte
des banques centrales des deux Etats;

(8) d'examiner tous les traités de commerce afin de ren-
dre possible l'unification du système des traités de
commerce des deux Etats;

(9) d'examiner toutes les questions concernant l'union
douanière, et de donner son avis à leur sujet en les
présentant aux Gouvernements respectifs.

Article 7

Tous les projets de lois unifiées et tous les projets de conventions élaborés en application des dispositions de l'article
6 du présent Traité par les soins de la Commission générale,
seront présentés aux Gouvernements respectifs et ils n'entreront en vigueur qu'après leur adoption par les institutions législatives des deux Etats et l'échange des instruments de ratification respectifs.

Toutes les autres décisions de la Commission générale
prises en vertu de l'article 6 n'exigent pour leur mise en
vigueur que l'approbation des deux Gouvernements.

Article 8

Les travaux prévus par l'article 6 p. 1 doivent être exécutés dans un délai d'un an à compter du jour de l'entrée
en vigueur du présent Traité.

Il est toutefois entendu qu'en cas de nécessité et si les
deux Gouvernements y consentent, la présentation du tarif
douanier commun aux institutions législatives peut être
ajournée par six mois.

Tous les autres travaux prévus par l'article 6 doivent être
exécutés dans un délai permettant de présenter aux institu-

tions législatives les projets respectifs de lois ou de conventions en temps convenable pour que la ratification et
l'échange des documents de ratification puissent être effec-
tués pendant les 3 annés qui suivront le jour de l'entrée en
vigueur du tarif douanier unifié.

La Commission générale a, toutefois, le droit, en ce qui
concerne l'unification des lois visées dans l'article 6, à l'exception du tarif douanier commun, de décider quelles dispositions des lois respectives pourront rester non unifiées,
ou de prolonger temporairement le délai de leur unification.
Les décisions susmentionnées de la Commission générale
entreront en vigueur après leur approbation par les deux
Gouvernements. Toutefois, la non-exécution des travaux
visés dans lesdites décisions ou leur prolongation tempo-
raire n'empêche pas l'entrée en vigueur de l'union douanière dans le délai fixé par l'article 1.

Tous les délais prévus dans le présent article pourront
être prolongés, mais seulement d'un commun accord entre
les deux Gouvernements.

Article 9

Les taux du tarif douanier commun doivent être fixés
en francs-or et pour le payement des droits de douane
l'Esthonie acceptera la Eesti-kroon or sur base de parité
(1 : 0.72009).

Les banques d'émission des deux Etats échangeront le
lats contre la Eesti-kroon sur base de parité or sans perception de commission.

Article 10

Les litiges ou divergences d'opinion entre les deux Parties Contractantes sur l'application et l'interprêtation du
présent Traité seront tranchés par un tribunal arbitral
mixte. Le tribunal arbitral sera constitué *ad hoc* et devra
comprendre un nombre égal de représentants des deux parties. Si ces représentants ne parviennent pas à se mettre
d'accord, ils feront appel à un tiers-arbitre neutre dont la
désignation, à défaut d'accord entre les deux Parties, sera

demandée au Président de la Cour Permanente de Justice Internationale.

Article 11

Sans attendre l'exécution du présent Traité, les deux Parties Contractantes procèderont à l'élaboration d'un traité économique provisoire tendant à faciliter la circulation des produits du sol, de l'agriculture et de l'industrie des deux pays avant même que l'union soit réalisée.

Article 12

Le présent Traité sera ratifié et les ratifications en seront échangées à Tallinn. Il entrera en vigueur le jour de l'échange des instruments de ratification.

Le présent Traité reste en vigueur pendant dix ans à compter de la date prévue par l'art. 1. Ce terme expiré, il restera en vigueur pendant les deux ans qui suivront le jour de sa dénonciation par l'une des Parties Contractantes.

Fait en double expédition en français et signé à Riga, le 5 février 1927.

(L.S.) Fr. Akel.   (L.S.) F. Cielens.

PROTOCOLE FINAL

Ad art. 2. (1) Il est entendu que la faveur du traitement national accordée réciproquement aux ressortissants de l'autre Etat au sujet du droit d'établissement ne deviendra applicable qu'à compter du jour de l'entrée en vigueur de l'Union douanière entre les deux Etats. Quant au temps précédant le terme visé ci-dessus les deux Gouvernements s'engagent à accorder réciproquement, en ce qui concerne le droit d'établissement, le traitement de la nation la plus favorisée.

(2) Les dispositions de l'article 2 du présent Traité ne seront pas considérées comme dérogeant aux dispositions de l'art. 18 de la convention de frontière en date du 19 octobre 1920 et de l'art. 6 de la Convention com-

plémentaire de frontière en date du Ier novembre 1923,
en ce qui concerne la liquidation des biens immeubles
partagés par la ligne de frontière.

Riga, le 5 février 1927.

(L.S.) Fr. Akel.   (L.S.) F. Cielens.

IX

LETTER OF CARDINAL GASPARRI, SECRETARY OF STATE OF THE HOLY SEE, TO CARDINAL DUBOIS, ARCHBISHOP OF PARIS

(This manifestation of Papal thought means of course much
more than the simple condemnation of a new book of French
nationalist authors, when it says that their ideals are "contrary
to the real catholic spirit.")

Ussita, le 28 aout 1927.

Eminentissime Seigneur,

Avec un retard inévitable, me sont parvenus dans cette
relative solitude, d'abord la nouvelle, ensuite, dans la *Se-
maine religieuse de Paris,* le texte de la condemnation que
Votre Eminence a portée contre le livre *L'Action française et le Vatican,* tout dernièrement publié par Ch. Maur-
ras et L. Daudet.

Votre Eminence a bien raison de penser et de dire qu'un
pareil livre peut faire beaucoup de mal.

Il peut le faire et presque inévitablement il doit le faire
à ceux qui *jurant in verba* de tels maîtres, comme aussi à
tous ceux qui n'ont aucun moyen de mettre les choses à
leur place et les voir sous leur vrai jour, grâce au système
suivi avec tant d'obstination, et même accentué dans ce
nouveau livre, malgré les paroles réitérées du Souverain
Pontife; système, dis-je, de changer et de déplacer sans
cesse la question du terrain religieux au terrain politique,
national et international; en prêtant aux personnes, aux
paroles et aux faits, des intentions, des significations ainsi

que des rapports, qui n'ont jamais existé; en cherchant, je ne saurais si plus hypocritement ou plus effrontément, à couvrir, sous de mensongères expressions de respect et de soumission, de véritables et très graves irrévérences, poussées jusqu'à l'insulte, à la désobéissance et à la révolte ouverte.

Tout ce que dit Votre Eminence pour motiver cette condamnation publique peut bien suffire pour faire comprendre à tous, et spécialement à ceux qui veulent être de vrais et bons catholiques, ce qu'ils doivent penser de ce livre, et comment ils doivent régler leur conduite à ce propos.

Le Saint Père désire que Votre Eminence voie dans ce que je lui écris sa satisfaction et sa pleine approbation pour la condamnation qu'elle a portée sur un livre qui, dans un sens très vrai, est tout ce qu'il y a de plus étranger et même de plus contraire à l'esprit vraiment catholique et romain.

Daigne Votre Eminence agréer l'assurance de la profonde vénération avec laquelle, en lui baisant les mains, j'ai l'honneur de me déclarer,

DE VOTRE EMINENCE,
le très humble et très obéissant serviteur,
P. CARD. GASPARRI.

X

THE AUSTRIAN ATTEMPT TO MAKE A SEPARATE PEACE IN 1917

The allusion contained in chapter III (p. 35) to the famous letter of the Austrian Emperor to his brother-in-law Prince Sixte of Bourbon to get a separate peace for Austria, provoked a protest from the said prince, denying: (a) that the Austrian proposal meant the breaking of the Entente treaties with Italy; (b) that the German Emperor was cognizant of the *démarche*.

On his arrival in Europe, back from America, Count Sforza answered by the following letter, which appeared in the European press on the last days of September, 1927.

"Rentré de New-York en Europe par Anvers, je vois les *Débats* du 14 avec la lettre du prince Sixte de Bourbon.

"Ainsi que je le fais constamment, je ne releverai aucune allusion personnelle.

"Je ne perdrai même pas de temps à reévoquer ce qu'aurait pu être pour l'Italie l'offre de l'Empereur Charles. On le tira assez au clair à Saint-Jean-de-Maurienne.

"Le point nouveau est mon affirmation que les chefs de la guerre allemande connaissaient la démarche du souverain austro-hongrois. Le prince Sixte de Bourbon le nie. Sa bonne foi est, certes, absolue; j'ajoute même que beaucoup, presque tous, et des plus haut placés, l'ignorèrent, et en Allemagne et en Autriche.

"Cela s'était déjà vu: très probablement Bethmann-Hollweg ignora la violence fatale de l'ultimatum autrichien à la Serbie; qui ne l'ignorait pas était l'ambassadeur allemand à Vienne, Tchirski, ni les cercles militaires et dynastiques qu'il informait au-dessus de la chancellerie. Ce sont les avantages des gouvernements à politique personnelle. . . .

"Le prince Sixte de Bourbon dit très justement que ce qui importe, à présent, c'est de 'parer aux dangers,' etc. Mais—tout est là—si on croit que l'Autriche impériale était digne de vivre, et que c'est grand dommage qu'elle ne vive plus, cela signifierait que les Etats successeurs, Tchécoslovaquie, Yougoslavie, Roumanie agrandie, ne sont pas des entités à la vie sûre, des éléments essentiels de l'Europe de demain. Ils ne seraient que des constructions diplomatiques. C'est—paraît-il—l'avis de Lord Rothermere, et de quelques autres.

"Croyez, etc. . . .

SFORZA."

INDEX

Tewfik Pasha and London Supreme Council in 1921, 62, 63
Thiers, Adolphe, 15
Tommasini (Francesco) and Polish situation in 1920, 21, 26
Trentino, 29
Trialism, 37
Trieste and Austro-German propaganda during war, 29; and frontier line, 42
Tripartite Agreement, 63, 104
Trumbich, Ante, 37, 39, 41, 101, 102
Turkey, 51, 54, 56, 57, 62, 104, 105

United States and Russia, 73

Vatican, 33, 34, 82, 86, 87, 90, 91, 92, 95, 96
Venizelos, Eleutherios, 57, 61, 62

Versailles, Treaty of, 1, 2, 5, 10, 17, 22, 24, 30, 90
Vesnich, 101, 102
Vienna, Congress of, 2, 3, 5

Weygand's (General) Strategical advice to Polish army, 21
Wilhelmina, Queen, 89
William II and his rhetorical phrases, 31, 32
Wilson, Sir Henry, 57
Wilson, Woodrow, and the two faces of the Versailles Treaty, 5, 6, 7

Yugoslavia, see Serbs, Croats, and Slovenes, Kingdom of the

Zara, annexed to Italy, 42
Zita, ex-Austrian Empress, and her Bourbon blood, 35

327.4
5523

Date Due

Aug 19 '47			
Mar 20 04			